MW00938092

Volumes of Praise
For A Vanishing God

To Richard and Leona,
Grace, mercy, and peace,
David Steen

By the same author:

Worship and Congregational Singing

(Fall, 2015)

Volumes of Praise
For A Vanishing God

The Growing Space Between
The Historic Faith and Modern Worship Music

David F. Neu

NeuSong, LLC
2015

Copyright © 2015 by NeuSong, LLC

All rights reserved. This book or any portion thereof may not be reproduced or used in any manner whatsoever without the express written permission of the publisher except for the use of brief quotations in a book review or scholarly journal.

First Printing, 2015

ISBN 978-1-329-25567-8

NeuSong, LLC
9260 Yarrow Street, Unit C
Westminster, CO 80021

www.neusong.com

Ordering information:

Special discounts are available on quantity purchases by churches, educators, associations, and others. For details, contact NeuSong, LLC, at the above address.

U.S. trade bookstores and wholesalers: Please contact NeuSong, LLC. Telephone: 303-463-4063 or 805-689-1991 (mobile); or contact us via email at: distribution@neusong.com.

Dedication

To

Karen

An excellent wife, who can find?
For her worth is far above jewels.

Proverbs 31:10

Contents

Acknowledgements

The project that has led to the two books, *Worship and Congregational Singing*, and the present volume, has taken far longer than I ever anticipated. The sustained encouragement of several colleagues and friends has been a great help in keeping me "at it." Special recognition is due my Westmont College colleagues, mathematician Russell Howell and philosopher Stanley Obitts, for hours of discussion, and in the case of Professor Obitts, the enormous amount of work he did in critiquing a draft of *Worship and Congregational Singing*, the fruit of whose work permeates both volumes. I am indebted also to Roger and Alexandra Pierce, new friends and fellow retired academicians, in theatre arts and music (composition and piano) respectively, for their reading of a recent draft.

Others who have played a large role include Eddie Almeida, his wife Susie, and the members of their congregation who have endured a large number of my lectures on various aspects of the subject. To these and the many others who have been a help and encouragement over these years, I express my deepest thanks. Also, to Lisa Guest for her fine editorial work on the present volume. The insightful cover design is the work of Susan Robbins

ix

and Bill Barrison; my thanks to them as well. Jim Ingle has been most helpful in preparing the music for neusong.com and in rendering other technical assistance. Matt Simonsen and his company Khoza Technology have been most gracious in hosting my website, neusong.com, as well as in helping me in its on-going development.

As is always the case, the author bears the final responsibility for the book, its contents and conclusions. Given the controversial nature of the subject, it will come as no surprise to learn that the personal convictions of those who have helped me, range from disagreement to strong endorsement of my conclusions. Their contributions have been valuable nonetheless.

I would be remiss if I failed to acknowledge the life-changing role of my college organ mentor, Charles H. Finney (1912–1995), Fellow of the American Guild of Organists, who graciously allowed me to continue as an organ minor in spite of the fact that he had responsibility for a large group of organ majors, who were much more deserving of his time and attention than I. It was he who, by precept and example, quickened my interest in congregational singing and the importance of competent accompaniment.

Special thanks to my loving wife, Karen, who has steadfastly and enthusiastically stood beside me through many decades including these years devoted to the research and writing of these books. Throughout my career in teaching mathematics in Christian colleges, her lovely soprano voice and enthusiasm for sharing our love of hymnody, have provided the leadership for countless hymn-sings with college students. In addition, we have spent hours in profitable discussion of the ideas that have come out of the research. She has read many drafts of both volumes, keeping me from straying too far from my intended audience. Even though the work has consumed what is surely the major part of our retirement years, her unwavering conviction that this work must be completed has been a great encouragement to me. For her love and support I will be forever grateful.

Preface

Although my career was devoted to mathematics, my retirement years have been given over to the study of a different subject, namely, congregational singing. As a music minor in college, I had the great privilege of studying with the outstanding organist Charles H. Finney. My subsequent years of service as a church organist coincided with the dramatic change in the evangelical church's congregational singing, from the dominance of the gospel song style to the almost exclusive use of contemporary Christian music. This experience kept alive a question I had first wondered about in college: Is there a biblical basis for answering the fundamental questions about the music used for congregational singing?

This book is a partial answer to that question. A more complete answer can be found in my book *Worship and Congregational Singing*. The present volume is a much less ambitious undertaking. The motivation for this narrower focus, as well as for the title, comes from the Preface to *The Knowledge of the Holy: The Attributes of God; Their Meaning in the Christian Life*, by A. W. Tozer, published shortly before his death in 1963.[1] Tozer wrote this:

1. Tozer, A. W. *The Knowledge of the Holy: The Attributes of God; Their Meaning in the Christian Life*. New York: Harper & Row, 1961.

> The message of this book does not grow out of these times but it is appropriate to them. It is called forth by a condition which has existed in the Church for some years and is steadily growing worse. I refer to the loss of the concept of majesty from the popular religious mind. The Church has surrendered her once lofty concept of God and has substituted for it one so low, so ignoble, as to be utterly unworthy of thinking, worshipping men. This she has done not deliberately but little by little and without her knowledge; and her very unawareness only makes her situation all the more tragic.

It is well-known that the twentieth century, even before the time of contemporary Christian music, yielded a very large collection of Christian songs, and that many, particularly gospel songs, were increasingly heard via phonograph recordings and on Christian radio broadcasts even in the first part of the century. Tozer's observation regarding the decline of the church's conception of God during the same period, underscored conclusions I had arrived at through work on *Worship and Congregational Singing*. Being convinced that the same patterns continue to hold early in the twenty-first century, I concluded that a book examining the relationship between what the church is singing and how it views God, would be appropriate to these times. The title, "Volumes of Praise for a Vanishing God," seemed most fitting.

Not only is the focus of this book narrower than that of *Worship and Congregational Singing*, it is also less an academic study and therefore more accessible. The ideas, however, are still non-trivial. Herein I deal only with the music of congregational singing, not the texts. As will become obvious as we proceed, the primary emphasis is on the question of contemporary Christian music vs. the traditional gospel song vs. the classic hymn tune.

On only a few occasions is the location of a quotation given. For this choice I can be justly faulted, but the decision was made in order to keep the presentation as unimposing as possible. *Worship and Congregational Singing* contains all the source information, as well as more detailed argumentation and examples. Also in that book are abundant endnotes on aspects of the subject that some might see as tangential if they were included in the text itself.

Terms that are either used in a technical sense or are frequently misunderstood, are defined in the Glossary. The first appearance of each is preceded and followed by asterisks. For example, the term *"gospel song"* is not well understood in the evangelical community. It is, in fact, often thought to be synonymous with *"hymn."* Therefore, the first use of *"gospel song"* in the text of the book proper appears as *gospel song*.

When a song title appears in italic type, the reference is to both the text (lyrics) and the music to which it is commonly sung in the United States. In the case that only the text is intended, the name is given in Roman type in quotation marks.

In this volume I do include several musical examples, some as short as two chords, others as long as a line of a hymn tune. These can be heard (repeatedly, if desired) on the website www.neusong.com. (At the main menu just select "Book Information," "Volumes of Praise," and then "Examples." You will be asked for the chapter number and the figure number of the desired example.)

At times, I will invite you to sing a familiar set of words to a tune that might not be commonly used for that text. (You can do this by locating the text in a song book or online, and then going to the above website, but instead of chapter and figure numbers you can request the tune by the name given in the book.) For example, more than once I refer to the text "O Sacred Head, Now Wounded," which can be found in most church hymnals, but I suggest that the words be sung to the tune Webb, which is the name by which musicians speak of the music that almost always accompanies the text, "Stand Up, Stand Up for Jesus." (To act on this suggestion, just obtain a copy of the words and then go to the website and ask for the tune Webb.)

In order to keep the book as short and straightforward as possible I have limited the number of examples. A good case in point is the repeated reference to "O Sacred Head" sung to Webb. I could generate countless examples of bad matches of text and music, but I know of none that is more glaring than this one. Hence there is no need for discussion of subtlety. Those interested in subtlety on one point or another will find plenty in *Worship and Congregational Singing.*

Soli Deo Gloria

David F. Neu
Westminster, CO

Chapter 1

What this book is about

The past half-century has been a time of great musical turmoil in much of the evangelical church. For a number of reasons, some of which I will discuss later, one's stylistic taste in the secular pop music arena has become a major influence in the lives of many young people. Musical preference is held so tenaciously that when churchgoing young people need to decide what church to attend, the style of music used in the worship service becomes a prime consideration.

At the same time, there are many people in the church who grew up in an earlier time and came to cherish more traditional music. Moreover, they typically do not listen to secular pop music, and so they are unfamiliar with it. From them one frequently hears complaints that contemporary Christian music is too loud, has too heavy a beat, and has no discernible melody. They also find it unsettling that the songs are sung over and over again but only for a brief time before they are set aside in favor of newly-written ones.

This contentious time has come to be known to many as the "music wars." One has to sympathize with the church leadership who have been trapped between opposing sides. On the one hand, the future of the church depends on a constant infusion of young people. On the other hand, it is the older members of a church who offer the financial resources, who serve on the various boards of the church, and provide continuity in mission and message. What's a pastor to do?

Unfortunately, rather than getting at the root of the musical wars issue, the church has developed some ways to try to reduce the tension. Three approaches to the problem have become common. One method is to have separate services for the different musical preferences, the "traditional" service vs. "contemporary" service idea, with which we have all become familiar.

The second method is a variation of the first. In this model the congregation separates into smaller groups according to musical taste. The different groups meet in separate rooms at the same hour and sing songs in the style they prefer. At the appointed time attention in each group turns to a screen mounted in the front of the room and everyone on the campus hears the same sermon or teaching via closed-circuit TV. This is essentially the same as having separate services (at different times) with the same pastor preaching the same sermon at each one.

The third approach is called the "blended service." Here the single worship service includes some contemporary and some traditional songs, so that the "pain" of having to endure music that is not of one's preference is shared across the congregation. However, this approach only "papers over" the problem. During the singing of a given song, some will be unwilling or unable to enter into it wholeheartedly, and the lack of unity among the worshipers, though perhaps less obvious, is still present.

All three of these methods share a common weakness in that each fails to represent the great New Testament value: *the unity of the Church.* The image of oneness of the body of believers was a primary concern in the early church. It was so important that the Church Fathers insisted that the congregation sing in unison so that the many might be heard as speaking with one voice.

It must be understood that the spiritual unity of the believers is not in doubt, for that spiritual unity is the work of the Holy Spirit and nothing that humans can do will add to it or detract from it. In this book, the concern with these different approaches to music is that each implicitly denies that corporate worship should be conducted in a manner that is consistent with the revealed truth of God, in this case, a manner that symbolizes the unity of all believers.

Divisions within the church are understandable if they arise out of fundamental theological disagreement. Understandable, but yet lamentable. Such divisions are often the result of inescapable human limitations on knowledge, especially as we seek to probe divine mysteries such as free will vs. election.

Separations in the church that arise out of mere personal preference are more difficult to justify. After all, when joining a local church everyone has to compromise on numerous preferences, some, perhaps, dearly held. We do so for a greater good, that being to represent the unity of believers. The truth of the oneness of the Church occupies such a high place in the theology of the apostle Paul, for example, that we would do well to see it as a "good" far greater than personal preferences. Whenever possible the unity of the body of believers should be symbolically represented in our worship.

Of course, the unanswered question here is: Where on the scale that runs from "fundamental theological disagreement" to "mere personal preference" does the choice of musical style fall? Answering that question is a major focus of this book. Is it true—as many believe—that the musical style of congregational singing is entirely a matter of personal preference? Or, is there something of far greater theological importance that needs to be considered?

Within a church, divisions based on musical preference can have consequences that go well beyond just destroying the symbol of unity, important though that is. Many of these sub-divisions of the congregation will use one musical genre or style exclusively, one that is tied to a particular historical period. For example, the *gospel song*, so cherished by today's older churchgoers, is firmly rooted in the nineteenth and early twentieth centuries, while contemporary Christian music is of even more recent origin. Singing just the music of one era undermines not only the picture of unity in today's church, but it also dims our awareness of our oneness with past generations of believers.

And there is *more* to be considered. From generation to generation the church's theological emphases tend to shift. In the late eighteenth, nineteenth, and early twentieth centuries, a significant segment of America's evangelicals was focused on salvation, revivalism, strong emotionalism, and the second-coming of Christ. Many in this group scorned formal theological education, even for preachers, and—not surprisingly—had little interest in theological systems, like Calvinism. In every sense, a populist movement had arisen within evangelicalism.

It was in those days that America experienced the second Great Awakening, the Campmeeting movement, and, later, the Dwight Moody/Ira Sankey and Billy Sunday/Homer Rodeheaver revivals. This emphasis on revivalism and the diminished interest in theology naturally influenced the texts of the Christian songs composed in those days, primarily the gospel song. In the large number of churches that used the gospel song to the virtual exclusion of other, older songs of the Church, the worshipers naturally came to focus on those same subjects. Important theological truths tended to be easily passed over.

Supreme among these neglected truths is that of the resurrection of Jesus Christ. This statement will surprise many Christians, for we all confess our faith in the bodily resurrection of our Savior. The problem comes when we realize that there has been such strong emphasis on the substitutionary death of Christ and the need for a person to place his/her faith in that atoning death, that we have lost to a large degree the emphasis of the New Testament and the early church on the resurrection. Naturally, this theological weakness ultimately shows up in the texts of our songs. We glibly sing, "It is enough that Jesus died and that He died for me," and the very recent line, "Here in the death of Christ I live." Implied is the idea that the death of Christ for sin is all that is needed. To this the Apostle Paul would cry out, "No!" Without His bodily resurrection we would have nothing! (1Corinthians 15:14).

The same phenomenon is happening now in the nearly-exclusive use of contemporary Christian music in worship. Without delving into the causes of these new emphases, we can clearly see that basic biblical concepts that the Church has held to for centuries have been shunned by preachers and are missing from the texts of the contemporary songs. Virtually gone is any emphasis on the all-important resurrection of Christ, or on sin, judgment, eternal damnation, holiness of life, sacrifice of one's ambitions for the sake of the kingdom of God, etc. In their place there is a heavy emphasis on "relationship" with God. When the songs that people sing, or listen to, for hours each week fail to mention Christian fundamentals like these, they become dim in the minds of the congregation.

But there is even more about which to be concerned when the people of God are content to sing songs from a rather narrow, recent period of time in church history. These effects have to do not with the texts but with the music. They are much more subtle than those that arise out of the song texts. The exploration of these musical effects is a prime topic of this book.

Clearly, this lack of emphasis on what the Church has historically believed and practiced weakens our present-day theological moorings. We are seeing many examples of this today as long-held doctrines, such as sin, reverence before God, faith in His word, etc., are set aside, some because they are offensive to the "modern mind," others because our conception of God has been corrupted.

Two missing pieces in evangelicalism

The inability to find a real solution to the music wars has exposed two rather large missing pieces in evangelicalism. *The first is that there is no consensus as to the nature, and the purpose, or even the importance of, corporate worship.* Some scholars, for instance, have concluded that worship in the New Testament era extends to all of daily life, and so there is no compelling need for a worship service. True, the church ought to get together, but they could gather for fellowship or instruction, etc., instead of worship.

Among churches today that maintain a regular "worship service," the goal of that gathering varies widely. A few churches hold to the idea that worship centers on the contemplation and celebration of the glory of God. More popular today is the service focused on edification through Bible teaching. A few churches design the service as an evangelistic outreach. Others see a worship service as a time for encouraging one another in living the Christian life, or simply as a time for fellowship with other believers. Finally, more than a few critics argue that modern worship is little more than a time of entertainment for the congregation.

A rather curious trend has developed in recent years, and that is the use of the word "*worship*" to reference an extended time of congregational singing. For example, in churches that emphasize Bible teaching, one often hears the song service described as "worship," and the lecture or sermon as "teaching."

In addition to meaning different things by the word *worship*, the church does not agree on the one toward whom worship should be directed. Earlier, one insightful evangelical leader lamented that even in his day the worship of the church was very often aimed "squarely at the man in the pew." If that was true in the 1950s, many would say that it is more so today.

Frequently Christian young people have gone off to college and, perhaps for the first time, faced the question of which church they'll attend. It is not at all uncommon to hear them say after their visit to a worship service, "It didn't do anything for me," or, "I didn't get anything out of it." It would not be far from the mark to claim that many churchgoers, young and old, think of the service in terms of what they get out of it. In short, they see the congregation—they see themselves—as the audience.

So, basic questions about worship remain unsettled, as do a host of questions about the role of congregational singing. This brings us to the second great missing piece in evangelicalism: *there is no agreement about the style of music appropriate to church or about the place of music in the church.*

Even among a group that agrees on what worship should be, rarely are there given any well-reasoned answers to fundamental questions about congregational singing. For example, what does congregational singing accomplish? Is its primary role to give the worshipers an emotional boost? Is singing so important that it's worth all this trouble? Are we sure that we're not doing more harm than good by singing?

And the questions continue. There's another question, one that strikes at the heart of congregational singing. Is the whole point of singing to increase the zeal, or ardor, with which the texts are uttered? We will see that this is a worthy goal, provided that the impetus toward greater passion is carefully managed. If it is not, then the worshipers are in danger of hypocrisy—of, in effect, appearing that they are more zealous for what they are saying than they really are. Such dishonesty should have no part in the worship of the God of truth.

And then the question touched on initially in this chapter: Is it really true that the style of music doesn't matter so long as the words are biblically sound? It is widely held—practically an article of faith—that the music itself has no meaning, and so the choice of style is simply a matter of one's preference. This is used to justify an "anything goes" attitude toward the music of congregational songs. But is it that simple? Suppose that this "article of faith" isn't true. Then what?

What, then, is the goal of this book?

Simply put, my goal is to develop a biblical foundation for congregational singing in order to find reliable answers to these questions. I discuss at length the large questions of the nature and purpose of worship, the symbolism of unity in worship, and the concerns about song texts, in my more expansive book, *Worship and Congregational Singing*. In these pages, my focus is on the *music* used in congregational singing, with only scant attention given to the texts.

This will be only a "bird's-eye view" of the subject of congregational singing. Again, those who prefer a more detailed presentation will find it in *Worship and Congregational Singing*.

Chapter 2

Why do we sing in worship?

Congregational singing has become so commonplace in evangelical worship services that it might seem odd to ask why we do it. Our search for a biblical foundation should begin with a brief history.

In the early church the worshipers sang mostly from the Psalms but also sang a few songs such as doxologies that were biblical but not quotations of Scripture. During the Middle Ages when Roman Catholicism held sway in Western Europe, the singing was done primarily by the officiating priest and the choir.

It was not until the Protestant Reformation in the early sixteenth century that congregations began to sing again. Martin Luther (1483–1546), the great reformer, is credited with restoring congregational singing. However, the truth is that, while not opposed to it, he was hardly a champion of it. His greater interest was in encouraging people to sing in the home and at school. In his evangelical Latin Mass (1523), the choir and priest did most of the singing; congregational singing was limited. That Mass remained the principal service in Luther's church in Wittenberg, Germany, for the rest of his life. If he had been dissatisfied with it, he certainly could have changed it.

Another of the leaders of the Reformation was Huldrych Zwingli (1484–1531), who lived in Zurich, Switzerland. He had been trained for a career in music yet he argued—quite persuasively, judging by the results—that in worship, music is a great distraction. Zwingli wrote, "It is against all human reason, that one is thoughtful or devout amid great bustle and noise." In short, he was opposed to all music in the worship service. Thus, these two great early reformers, Luther and Zwingli, had very different views on the appropriateness of music in the worship service. The historian, Charles Garside, Jr., wrote, "For Luther music was to be an essential, indeed an indispensable, element of worship. For Zwingli, on the other hand, music was to be excluded entirely from worship."

About five years after Zwingli's death in 1531, the third of the great reformers, John Calvin (1509–1564), began his ministry in Geneva, Switzerland. He was the least musical of the three, and, at first, was probably closer to Zwingli's position regarding music in worship than he was to Luther's. However, during his first year in Geneva, Calvin was dismayed by the coldness and lack of zeal with which the worshipers engaged in congregational recitations. Knowing of the warmth of the singing in the Strasbourg, France, church of another reformer, Martin Bucer (1491–1551), Calvin quickly changed his position from indifference toward congregational singing to insistence on it.

Calvin, however, allowed only the singing of *metricized* Psalms and some other biblical passages, such as the Ten Commandments. In doing so he thought that he was following the pattern of the early church, evidently unaware of the fact that some texts not taken directly from Scripture were used in the early centuries. Ultimately, one-third to one-half of the time in Calvin's worship service was given to congregational singing.

In contrast to Calvin, Luther encouraged the use of texts of "human composure" that were faithful to Scripture but not necessarily direct quotations of it. As such, they were often referred to as "uninspired texts."

So, even with the rebirth of congregational singing during the Reformation, leaders disagreed about what, if anything, should be sung in worship. As Chapter 3 will reveal, controversy, to one degree or another, has attended congregational singing throughout the history of the church. Perhaps we need to look not only at the question: *Why do we sing in worship?* but to ask also: *Should we sing in worship?*

This chapter deals with the question of why we sing in worship and explores some potential benefits of singing. In Chapter 3, we will discuss the other side of the coin: Should we even be singing in worship? There we will see some ways in which singing can disrupt worship.

Some potential benefits

Congregational singing offers at least four potential benefits:

1. Singing adds warmth and vitality to worship

Calvin embraced singing in worship in order to increase the zeal with which worshipers participated. Why would that be necessary?

If a single person were speaking from his/her heart, especially in declaring the glory of God, it would seem that there would be appropriate emotion. But it seems clear that when the entire congregation reads a text, something changes. Participants in a joint reading find it more difficult to respond emotionally to the text than if they each were reading it alone. There are several reasons for this.

If the whole congregation is participating then the text must have been prepared in advance by someone else. Unless we are already inclined to be thinking about the subject of the reading, it may take time for us to become fully engaged. In other words, we are probably not speaking "from the heart." This is even more the case if the text is not taken from Scripture but is, say, someone's paraphrase, and we have some reservations about it.

Moreover, participants in a joint reading can find it easy to let their attention slip ever-so-slightly. What can result is reading the words as individual words rather than contemplating the ideas. When that happens, the recitation will, indeed, become cold.

It is completely understandable that attention would slip, for in joint readings we have to give heed to what others are doing so that our voice will not "stick out." We have to pay attention to the congregational *cadence*, or pace, so that we don't run ahead or lag behind. The points at which we pause to catch our breath are often awkward.

Finally, during a congregational reading, there is no opportunity to stop and re-read a sentence in order to grasp its meaning more fully. It helps understanding if the reading is a familiar creed, for example, but with familiarity comes the tendency to become intellectually lazy.

These reasons alone are enough to explain why a congregational reading often seems cold and mindless. Furthermore, looking back over the foregoing list, it is difficult to see how putting the text to music is going to improve the situation. The emotion induced by the music and by the singing can easily give the illusion of greater zeal, but is it anything more than just an illusion? This brings us back to the question raised in Chapter 1: Are we being truthful before God, and our fellow worshipers, if the increased zeal isn't genuine? That is, if the emotion is not coming from our contemplation of the text, then aren't we being deceitful? If so, then we have only compounded the problem by adding a degree of dishonesty to the underlying coldness.

These are not idle concerns. Every worshiper has had the experience of enthusiastically singing a text without really giving any thought to its meaning. In fact, this probably happens more often than we would like to admit. So, unless we are able to deal with these problems we must conclude that singing may actually do more harm to our worship than good.

Fortunately, the story does not end there. As we progress through the book we will see that under certain conditions, singing can produce warmth *with integrity*.

2. Singing enables us to express our thoughts more fully

At times during a worship service our contemplation of who God is and what He has done can arouse significant emotion. The view espoused in this book is that this should be a frequent, even normal, experience in worship. According to the theoretical foundation for worship, to be laid out in Chapter 4, corporate worship should include a joint response by the congregation to what they have heard. To be an honest response it must accurately express the emotion that has been aroused. A congregational song might not be the only acceptable response, but if it is chosen carefully and sung thoughtfully, it surely ranks at the top of the list.

A couple of examples from our life as a nation will help to clarify this. No American will ever forget the horrific terrorist attacks on the United States on 9/11/2001. On a smaller scale, we also witnessed the devastating explosion of bombs at the finish line of the Boston Marathon on 4/15/2013. In the population as a whole, these two events prompted levels of emotion that are rarely seen on such a national scale.

In each case there was a very interesting response by some people who were most closely involved. Late in the day on 9/11, the leaders and many other members of the Congress of the United States gathered on the Capitol steps and sang *God Bless America*. On more than one evening after the Boston Marathon bombings, while the authorities were still engaged in trying to apprehend the bombers, groups of Boston citizens gathered spontaneously and joined in singing the *National Anthem*.

It is instructive to reflect on both why this was done and the manner in which it was done. Apparently when we are jointly feeling strong emotions, singing together is an effective way to express them.

But to be effective our singing must meet two conditions, both of which were met on each occasion. First, the song text must be seen as expressing the thoughts underlying the emotion. The song choices that were made in Washington and Boston were most appropriate. Contrast the effect if those gathered together had chosen, instead, to sing a different traditional American song such as *Yankee Doodle,* or *Dixie,* or *Home on the Range.* The texts of these songs have nothing to do with the thoughts that occupied the minds of Americans at the time. Those songs would have destroyed the effectiveness of the group singing.

Second, the music of the song must agree with the strength and type of emotion being experienced. Both of these patriotic songs have been sung in baseball parks before the game or at the seventh-inning stretch, and almost always they are embellished by the soloist in a contemporary popular style. But not on the occasions of the attacks. In both cases those songs were sung "straight." There was no embellishment, neither vocal nor instrumental. Any such embellishment would have compromised the sublime patriotism expressed by the simple singing.

These two conditions on the text—*Does the text express the thoughts underlying the emotion?* and music—*Does the music match the strength and type of emotion being experienced?*—of a song apply directly to congregational singing in a worship service.

3. Singing can help to unify the congregation's worship

When a congregation reads a text together there is a degree of unity evident. If the worshipers are careful to think about the text as they read it, then there is a unity of thought as well. Even though this cannot be observed by mortals, it is readily apparent to God, to whom our worship should be addressed.

If the text is put into the form of a song, and if the musical setting is well-chosen, then the singing of the text encourages a unity of emotion across the congregation. Thus, when done carefully, singing can bring to corporate worship the deepest unity: oneness in word, thought, and emotion.

4. Singing can strengthen the contemplation of the text

We have already seen that corporate recitation tends to draw our attention away from the text because of the demands of speaking in unison. It is easy to see that singing is even more demanding than this. For example, in addition to thinking about the cadence we must also pay attention to what the next note is, and aim to sing it correctly. This is especially problematic when singing contemporary songs because the congregation rarely sees the music, and brand-new songs, unknown to the congregation, are introduced with great frequency.

But the picture for singing is not all negative. It turns out that in order to speed up *cognitive processing*, the human mind is always preparing for what is likely to happen next. If its guess (or, prediction) is close to being right, then processing is faster and more mental resources can be devoted to thinking about, in this case, the meaning of the text. However, if the prediction is way off, then it takes time and resources for the mind to readjust and understand what is happening. In both reading and singing, new information keeps coming at a rapid pace, so that poor predictions will mean that little cognitive power is available for contemplating the text.

In congregational readings the worshipers have few clues as to what comes next, but we shall see that in singing, if the music "fits" the text well, then the mind of the worshiper can make better predictions. These better predictions can lead to a better understanding of the text. Of course, the operative phrase here is *"fits the text well,"* a phrase that we will unpack as we go through the book.

We have listed four benefits that congregational singing can bring to the worship service. These are not the only ones, but they are surely among the most important. Now comes the hard question.

Do we experience these benefits when we sing in church?

You may have noticed that each of these potential advantages of congregational singing has a condition attached to it. None of those conditions is automatically satisfied just because we sing. They all involve the music and how appropriate it is to the text.

To get an idea of what all this means, try this experiment with the much-respected text, "O Sacred Head, Now Wounded," which is still sung in many church services, especially in the season of Lent. The text comes from a long Latin poem thought to have been written by the brilliant twelfth-century monk, Bernard of Clairvaux (1091–1153). The text was translated into German by Paul Gerhardt (1607–1676) and then into English by James W. Alexander (1804–1859).

The text is almost always sung to the *hymn tune* called "Passion Chorale." I suggest that you find "O Sacred Head" in a hymnal or online, and first read the words several times. Then sing it to Passion Chorale. Hearing the music at www.neusong.com might be helpful.

Next, try singing the same text to the tune Webb, which is almost always used to accompany the text "Stand Up, Stand Up for Jesus." The text was written by George Duffield (1818–1888) and the tune was written by George J. Webb (1803–1887). Webb is a pretty good tune for Duffield's text, but you should find it highly inappropriate for "O Sacred Head." Try to articulate what it is that makes Webb such a poor choice for "O Sacred Head."

Granted, this is an extreme example, but it's a good step toward understanding what is meant here by "the music fits the text well." In most cases the question of "fit" is much more subtle than in this example. Nevertheless, with a little practice, people can often hear two different tunes for the same text and come to agree on which one fits the text better. This is true regardless of a person's musical background, or lack thereof.

It will become clearer that each of the potential benefits of singing requires a good fit between music and text. Thus the benefits are not to be taken for granted or thought to happen automatically. Unfortunately, the prevailing wisdom in the evangelical church is that the music makes no difference, that only the text is important.

As a result, in many cases the music to be used for a song is chosen not with careful attention to the text but simply because someone thought that the music sounded nice, or had a good beat, or a clever melody, etc. It follows that because of this indifference to the matching of text and music, singing in the evangelical church rarely brings the potential benefits.

In a brief aside here, we should note that the argument that only the text is important is often used for a different purpose. Many times complaints raised about the music today are met with the response, "But the text is good and that's what really matters." Closer inspection reveals that the text is not always that good. It might be a "word salad" of theological terms that gives the illusion of good quality but, in reality, has little or no content, or is simply erroneous. Nevertheless the song continues to be used because some people in the congregation really like the music—the high-sounding text serves merely as justification.

So, why do we sing in worship?

A variety of answers will be offered. Some people will shrug their shoulders and say, "It's always been done this way." Others will say, "Most Christians like to sing." A harsh critic might suggest that congregational singing is a good cover for another activity, such as when the choir leaves after the anthem, or when children are dismissed to their own service. Someone might even remark that the singing gives the congregation a chance to change position before listening to the sermon.

But I think that the most likely reason that congregational singing continues is simply because it adds emotion to congregational expression and people enjoy a pleasant emotional arousal. British psychiatrist Anthony Storr (1920–2001) wrote, "The fact is that human beings are so constituted that they crave arousal just as much as they crave its opposite, sleep."

Emotion in worship is also highly valued because we expect true worship to be accompanied by heightened emotion. Genuine worship involves the contemplation of the person and work of God, a glorious topic that cannot but lead to emotional arousal.

The error arises when these two statements are thought to be "the same" statement:

> If worship is genuine then there will be emotion.

> If there is emotion then the worship is genuine.

But the statements say very different things. In this case—and in paired statements like these—one might be true and the other false.

We deal with this many times a day. Consider this statement:

> If you run a red light, then you will be fined.

In a world of perfect law enforcement the statement would be true. Now consider the statement:

> If you are fined, then you ran a red light.

Even in an ideal world the statement is clearly nonsense—there are lots of other reasons why you or I might be fined.

So, too, with the statement: "If there is emotion then the worship is genuine." There are many easy ways to spark an emotional response even when the worship is clearly not genuine. False religions do this all the time.

Of even greater concern for the church's high valuation on emotional arousal is that, by one means or another, Christians have come to regard heightened emotion in a church service as evidence that the Holy Spirit is working in the hearts and minds of those present.

The logical error here is exactly the same one as we saw above. It may be true that:

> If the Holy Spirit is at work then there will be emotional arousal.

But that is very different than saying:

> If there is emotional arousal then the Holy Spirit is working.

The error of confusing emotion with the "movement of the Holy Spirit" has been in the church since at least the First Great Awakening (~1740).

Think about the fact that when progress in one's spiritual life is described in terms of making a certain decision, the encouragement toward making the "right" decision is often accompanied by quiet music that involves some standard emotion-inducing techniques. These techniques may be used with the best of intentions, but nevertheless they raise very serious questions about truthfulness and integrity.

Actually, there is more to the story here. It is known that if a person is given even a slight positive emotional inducement, whether it be consciously perceived or not, then he/she is more inclined to believe that a certain statement is true. For many years advertising companies have known this and have used subtle devices, such as slightly provocative dress, to make their ads more effective. Subtle devices can also impact decision-making in the church, but there the effectiveness of any such devices is greatly enhanced by the sense that the Holy Spirit is working.

These errors are so deeply ingrained in the thinking of Christians that when one is observing evident emotion in a worship service, it is almost impossible to avoid believing that the worship is genuine and that the Holy Spirit is at work.

Since emotional arousal has such power, it is not surprising that acceptable ways are sought by which to induce it. One of the best ways is congregational singing.

Chapter 3

Should we sing in worship?

In Chapter 2, four potential benefits of congregational singing were listed, but the conclusion was that, in general, much of the singing in the evangelical church fails to produce them. I suggested that in many cases a major reason why we sing in worship is that it boosts the emotional level of the congregation. While this pleases the worshipers, if the elevated emotion is not closely tied to the other aspects of worship (e.g., the text of the song being sung), then the sobering question of truthfulness is raised: we are uttering a text with a zeal that, supposedly, indicates how we view the text, but in fact, it is due to the "artificial" emotion induced by the music.

I also pointed out that aroused emotion in worship is very easily misinterpreted as confirmation of genuine worship, or—more specifically—as being a result of the presence and working of the Spirit of God. Thus, congregational singing can easily lead to one or all three errors: 1) if worshipers sing with emotional force that doesn't match what they really think about the text, then in that part of worship, truthfulness has been compromised; 2) the worshipers can be misled into believing their worship to be genuine; and, 3) the emotion aroused by singing might be attributed to the

Holy Spirit, when it is actually due to musical devices that heighten one's emotion.

It should be noted that these errors are difficult to avoid after the singing has started. With diligence and careful planning by the church leadership, however, the chance of these occurring can be reduced.

Consider now the following three reasons—and there are others—why we should approach the question of congregational singing with some caution.

Problems incurred in singing

The focus of this book is the music of congregational singing, but we should not ignore the controversies that have arisen over texts. One controversy that goes back to the early days of the Church centers on "texts of human composure." That is, with song texts that are not found in Scripture.

Groups, such as the Gnostics and Arians, that denied the divinity or humanity of Jesus, understood that congregational singing is a powerful vehicle for the introduction of heresy. Put some erroneous teaching together with a pleasing melody and the people will be singing it all through the week, hearing the heresy over and over again. To prevent this, many leaders in the early church prohibited the use of any texts not taken directly from Scripture.

The introduction of error can occur without malicious intent. This can happen when the authors of song texts are not well-trained in theology. Even with the best of intentions, "evangelical folklore"—ideas that have become somewhat common in the church, but have never been carefully examined—slip into the song texts. We have already quoted, for instance, song lines that suggest that the cross is sufficient for our salvation.

In other cases, error creeps in by the misuse of theological terms, like "*holiness,*" (in the plea, "Hide me in your holiness"), or the confusion of ideas (as in "Who would have thought that a Lamb could rescue the souls of men?"). Again, if the music is attractive then the questionable ideas gain an even greater foothold.

· So, there are textual concerns about the songs sung in worship, but more numerous are the problems having to do with the music. Here are eight problems that ought to make us a bit more cautious about singing in worship.

1. The music itself is almost guaranteed to draw the singer's attention away from the text to some degree. By their mannerisms or even their voices, those leading the singing—whether it be a song leader or a contemporary worship team—are apt to do the same.

2. The use of musical instruments can subtly, even sub-consciously, introduce into the mind of the singer thoughts alien to worship. The Church Fathers were aware of this, so they excluded from worship most musical instruments because they were used in pagan rites and in the immoral theatrical plays of the day.

Another reason for the Church Fathers' prohibition was that even though harmony—as we know it—had not yet been developed, it was customary in the secular world for accompanying instruments to play a musical line different from the melody. The church leaders feared that if the same were to be done in worship, then the symbolic unity of the singing would be weakened.

Although even today some denominations prohibit the use of instrumental accompaniment, the use of instruments is much more common. But arguably, in contemporary Christian music the selected instruments are chosen *because* of their use in secular pop music. This is a 180° turn from the position held in the early church. Worship leaders who have adopted the use of such musical instruments discount any effect that their secular associations might have on the mind of the singer. That is a troubling assumption.

3. Unless music and text are carefully matched, they will likely compete for an individual's cognitive resources, making it more difficult for the singer to pay attention to the text. This distraction can easily occur unconsciously. For example, you may realize in retrospect that you thought about the text "O Sacred Head, Now Wounded" less intently when singing it to Webb than to Passion Chorale.

4. Congregational singing had been a source of disunity in the church, even before the last half-century. Unless this disunity can be avoided, it might be better not to sing.

5. It is difficult to find competent musicians who, when playing for a worship service, will adopt the attitude of a servant. Furthermore, hardly any single factor is more harmful to congregational singing than poor accompaniment. Obviously, an accompanist who makes mistakes frequently will cause a great distraction. But there are other errors that are less glaring, yet just as damaging. For example, playing too fast or too slow, or changing the tempo within the song at the whim of the accompanist, or trying to hurry the congregation along by leaving little time between verses. Such errors are heard routinely, even when the accompanist is a trained musician.

The difficulty is that solo musicians are accustomed to playing or singing a piece as they "feel" it. An uneven tempo might be perfectly appropriate in a solo performance, but not so when leading or accompanying a congregation. It is essential that the musician in worship set aside the prerogatives of the soloist and become a servant to the congregation and the text.

The same principle applies to song leaders, some of whom have fine voices and are accustomed to singing solos. Other song leaders are also choir directors who seem to think of the congregation as just a large choir. All too often such song leaders take liberties with the music—e.g., varying the tempo, shortening the duration of notes at the end of a line, leaving inadequate time between verses —and thereby introduce confusion.

And we must not overlook pastors who take it upon themselves to lead the congregational singing with their voices, often "jumping the gun" in starting a new line or a new verse.

These several mistakes can easily communicate to the congregation that the leader doesn't value singing all that much and would like to get it over with as quickly as possible. Or, these mistakes may indicate the simple desire to spur the emotions.

The moral of this story is: find a competent accompanist (not merely one who plays well) and let him/her lead the singing. The problem is the availability of such a person.

6. A great variety of musical preferences is usually represented in the congregation, and this reality will not go away with the passing of the present older generation, many of whom are lovers of the gospel song. It is very likely that when today's young people get into their middle years, the youth of that time will favor a newer style. The music wars will probably flare up again and again.

As we will see, a musical style that is unfamiliar does not help in a person's worship. What are worship leaders to do, then, when almost any style will be of little or no value for a significant portion of the congregation? One "solution" is to limit the singing to a particular musical style, and let the local Christian population sort itself out as each individual selects a church that comes closest to his/her musical preference. This is frequently done today, but it is fraught with unintended consequences, some of which we discussed in Chapter 1.

For a number of reasons a far better solution would be to come to understand that the worship of God demands a distinctively "churchly" musical style. What is meant by that will become clear as we progress through the book. But perhaps an immediate objection that will surely come to mind can be tackled now. The objection is: "If there are already so many styles represented in the congregation, what good will it do to bring in yet another?"

The answer is that the congregation must be patiently taught to appreciate the ability of this "churchly" style to enhance their worship through song. This learning process will not be just having everyone "grit their teeth" and sing in this style until, hopefully, they come to understand it. Such a hope is little more than wishful thinking.

The learning process will require more intentionality. Much can be done verbally, using abundant examples of "churchly" music, to open the eyes of people to a world that almost everyone can understand whether they have any musical training or not. When people begin to see that there are very substantial reasons for adopting this style in worship, most of the battle will have been won.

This education should not be a part of a worship service, though. Among the number of possible venues outside of worship in which to accomplish this are Sunday School classes, weekly fellowship meetings, and the internet.

7. Maintaining an appropriate level and type of emotional arousal via music is challenging. All too often emotion's seductiveness leads to excess. This problem can be managed by careful leadership in the choice of songs and style of accompaniment.

8. Finally, and most importantly, congregational singing makes it more difficult to keep the secular culture from seeping into, and ultimately destroying, the worship of God. We will see that the world's music can act like an insidious disease, subtly corrupting worship. As was said earlier, the Church Fathers were concerned about exactly that.

Others were concerned as well, among them the fourteenth century Pope John XXII (ruled 1316–1334). He issued a papal bull (decree) that sought to limit the introduction of music styles associated with secular music into the Catholic Mass. Up to that time the Gregorian chants had dominated the music of the Roman church. In the papal document, Pope John rejected not only current styles of the secular culture but also any that had not yet "lost their force in contemporary secular music." Evidently, he understood the destructive potential of music many centuries before music scholars laid the foundation for such concern.

The sixteenth-century Protestant reformers disagreed with one another over the use of *polyphonic* music, an eleventh-century style in which multiple "melodic" lines existed simultaneously in the music, as in a Bach fugue. (Polyphony was a primary motivation for Pope John's edict.) This form is different from the one most familiar to us, one in which there is, generally, one melody (usually the soprano line) and three other "supporting" lines (alto, tenor, and bass).

For his part, Reformer John Calvin strongly favored using in church a musical style distinct from that used in entertainment. In the *Preface to the Genevan *Psalter** of 1543, he wrote this:

> And in truth we know by experience that singing has great force and vigor to move and inflame the hearts of men to invoke and praise God with a more vehement and ardent zeal. Care must always be taken that the song be neither light nor frivolous; but that it have weight and majesty (as St. Augustine says), and also, there is a great difference between music which one makes to entertain men at table and in their houses, and the Psalms which are sung in the church in the presence of God and his angels.

Regarding music in the worship service, Martin Luther was less restrictive than Calvin, but the widely-circulated claim that he used the music of tavern songs has been thoroughly researched and shown to be without foundation.

Yet this baseless claim about Luther has been used repeatedly to defend the attitude of the contemporary church toward the music used in congregational singing. (It is interesting, but not surprising, that the contrary views of Calvin, as well as those of Zwingli, are ignored.) It is as though apostolic authority has been conferred upon Luther so that whatever he did or said has divine approval. Luther himself rejected any such status—and he hadn't used tunes from the bar anyway.

When the secular culture's music enters the church, we should not expect that its corrupting influence on the worship of God will be immediately apparent. Depending upon the nature of the influence, it may take several years, perhaps a decade or more, before the corruption is widely recognized. However, on the basis of church history and advances in our understanding of music, it may be possible to identify certain trends in the music of congregational singing as potentially damaging to our concept and worship of God.

One trend that is of particular relevance to this study is that, for the first time in the history of the Church, the musical styles of the secular popular culture are not merely seeping into worship, but rather are being wholeheartedly embraced. In fact a great number of evangelical churches have not only welcomed but have granted to the pop culture's musical styles virtually exclusive rights to use in the worship service. A primary goal in this book is to examine this phenomenon and assess its potential as a corrupting influence.

At this point, the description of these eight problems that arise when the congregation sings should suffice to raise serious doubts about the practice. History provides additional reasons for caution.

Some historical controversies over singing

We have already seen that controversy over congregational singing has been a problem since the beginning of the Church age. This chapter closes with a brief overview of two of the more contentious battles in what seems to be an unending music war. The emphasis of this book is on the issue of music style, but serious questions about the texts of contemporary songs also need to be asked. The following controversies give greater weight to textual issues, but involve music style at the point of *how* the songs were sung.

First, a bit of history. As was said earlier, disagreement over the use of "texts of human composure" goes all the way back to the very early centuries following the earthly ministry of Christ. As we saw in Chapter 2, the controversy flared again following the Protestant Reformation, when Calvin allowed the singing only of passages of Scripture suitably *metricized.*   Since the book of Psalms was the primary source of the biblical texts used, Calvin's position is often referred to as "*exclusive psalmody*."

Luther did not share Calvin's view. The Lutherans had a "head start." They began to write the texts of "spiritual songs" for use by the choir and in schools prior to 1524, whereas Calvin did not formulate his position on exclusive psalmody until the late 1530s.

As the Reformation spread from the continent to England and Scotland, Luther's position prevailed, at least initially. In 1553, after the death of King Edward VI, Mary (1516–1558), daughter of Henry VIII, became Queen Mary I, of England. She was intent on restoring Roman Catholicism as the official religion of the empire. To advance that cause she executed many Protestants, for which she came to be known as "Bloody Mary." In order to escape her wrath numerous Protestant leaders fled to the continent, many ultimately going to Geneva, where they came under the influence of Calvin.

When Mary died in 1558, her half-sister, Elizabeth (1533–1603), succeeded her and brought the reign of terror to an end. The "Marian exiles," including John Knox, then returned to England and Scotland, bringing with them the Calvinist emphasis on psalmody. Ultimately, under the influence of Knox, exclusive psalmody was officially adopted by the Scottish Church. The Church of England never formally adopted exclusive psalmody, but the singing of Psalms became the dominant position.

Controversy #1

In 1562, the complete English Psalter, metricized by Thomas Sternhold (1500–1549) and John Hopkins (dates unknown), was published in London. It was the prevailing psalter in England for more than a century. Many Christians memorized large portions of "Sternhold and Hopkins," which is today known as "The Old Version."

In an effort to reform the Church of England, the English Parliament convened the Westminster Assembly, which met from 1643 to 1652. In addition to producing the well-known *Westminster Confession* and the *Westminster Shorter Catechism*, the Assembly also recommended the use of a new psalter, known as "Rous's Version."

In 1696, the English Poet Laureate, Nahum Tate, and Dr. Nicholas Brady, created a new English psalter, "Tate & Brady," known also as "The New Version." Its poetry was more refined, but less literal, than that of "The Old Version." Tate & Brady became the chief competition for Sternhold & Hopkins, but was preeminent only in London and its environs.

In anticipation of a new psalter, and in view of the high rate of illiteracy among the populace, the Westminster Assembly instituted a method of congregational singing known as "lining-out the psalm." This approach called for a song leader, known as a precentor, to sing the first line of the psalm, after which the congregation would repeat what they had just heard; this alternation continued through the entire psalm.

"Lining out" led to a great controversy in congregational singing. Although intended only as a temporary aid to learning texts and tunes, lining-out became the dominant method of congregational singing throughout England and Scotland, as well as in the American colonies of New England. However, lining-out brought about a number of unexpected side-effects. For example, the congregation was often confused by precentors who exercised their assumed authority to embellish tunes, and in so doing to create new and very different versions of the same tune. Also, the singing was unaccompanied and so the worshipers, often unsure of what the precentor was going to do, waited to begin their part until they heard the pitch from him. That hesitation slowed the tempo significantly and the congregation had difficulty staying together. Also, the constant interruption of the text—listen to a line, sing the line; listen to a line, sing the line—made it difficult to maintain coherence of thought. It is difficult to understand why lining-out enjoyed such popular support.

This illustrates the fact that uncertainty in congregational singing always works to depress it. Not surprisingly, in the first part of the eighteenth century the state of congregational song in England and the American colonies could only be described as abysmal.

There was significant opposition to lining-out by those favoring a return to "regular singing." The conflict between the two sides became very intense in the 1720s, especially in New England. All manner of insults were hurled in both directions.

According to Cotton Mather (1663–1728), the famous New England Puritan minister and supporter of regular singing, the lining-out adherents accused the opposition of both bringing in popery and worshiping the devil. Mather charged that during regular singing, some favoring lining-out would run out of the meeting-house. Others either refused to sing or else tried to overwhelm the regular singers with the volume of their own singing.

In hindsight, some of the charges seem quite humorous. The following account appeared in the "New-England Courant," one of the first American newspapers:

> I am credibly inform'd, that a certain Gentlewoman miscarry'd at the ungrateful and yelling Noise of a Deacon [acting as Precentor] in reading the first Line of a Psalm: and methinks if there were no other Argument against this Practice (unless there were an absolute necessity for it) the Consideration of its being a Procurer of Abortion, might prevail with us to lay it aside.

The controversy over lining-out finally dissipated in New England with the First Great Awakening (~1740). Almost a century after the Westminster Assembly instituted it, lining-out yielded to regular singing.

Controversy #2

A second controversy was raging at about the same time that the people were debating the practice of lining-out. In 1679, seventeeen years before Tate & Brady was published, an English preacher by the name of John Patrick (1632(?)–1695) published his own partial psalter, which he later completed and published in 1691. His metrical versions of the Psalms were very different from those of Sternhold & Hopkins. Specifically, Patrick omitted some verses that were seen as thoroughly Jewish and not suited to New Testament doctrine (such as the passages that called upon God to pour out His wrath on one's enemies). In addition, Patrick used Christian (i.e., New Testament) language in several psalms where he thought it appropriate.

In other words, Patrick departed from the traditional standard of literalism when he translated from the Hebrew, and by doing so, he took a step in the direction toward paraphrasing the Psalms. Recall that Tate & Brady was less literal, but more refined poetically, than Sternhold & Hopkins. In evaluating Tate & Brady, some people were of the opinion that "paraphrased" would be an apt description for that work as well.

Thus, by the end of the seventeenth century new winds were blowing English psalmody in the direction of hymns of human composure. These breezes proved to be only the outer bands of an approaching hurricane that made landfall early in the eighteenth century with the publication of *Hymns and Spiritual Songs* (1707) and *Psalms of David Imitated* (1719) by Isaac Watts (1674–1748). In his words, the songs of the latter volume represent his efforts "to express myself as I may suppose *David* would have done, had he lived in the Days of *Christianity*." Clearly, Watts had paraphrased the Psalms.

Almost instantly the English-speaking Protestant church was engulfed in one of the fiercest storms ever experienced by the church, and the matter of congregational song was the reason. Many believers opposed Watts's texts, professing allegiance to traditional strictures against songs of human composure, but it is likely that for more than a few people, this profession was actually driven by a visceral attachment to Sternhold & Hopkins, whose dominance in congregational singing was threatened by the new songs. The controversy raged for scores of years, extending even into the nineteenth century in some places. Over time, Watts's hymns, as well as the songs of others who succeeded him, prevailed in most churches.

As Luther had done in Germany two centuries earlier, Watts opened the floodgate of extrabiblical songs in England and America. From that day to the present the torrent has continued, yielding both excellent texts, and, unfortunately, many others that are unworthy of use, not a few of which justify the early concerns of the church regarding the introduction of theological and doctrinal error.

Summary

In this chapter the question has been: *Should we sing in worship?* A list of problems that seem inevitably to attend congregational singing has been presented. In addition, we have looked briefly at the extended period of discord and contentiousness in the church that began in the late seventeenth century, a disunity due entirely to congregational song. The evidence in this chapter certainly weighs heavily toward a negative answer to the question: *Should we sing in worship?*

But we must not overlook the very strong potential benefits of congregational singing set forth in Chapter 2. Moreover, a closer look at the list of problems in this chapter suggests that they might not be as inevitable as they first appear. Most could be solved, or at least largely mitigated, by a few strategies that have already been suggested: the music must "fit" the text; the musical style (including the choice of instrumental accompaniment) should be distinctly "churchly"; and excessive emotional force in the music must be carefully avoided. Chapters 5–9 are devoted to a better understanding of these "strategies."

If these are faithfully and consistently implemented, the benefits of congregational singing listed in Chapter 2 are compelling enough to justify the considerable effort required. We should sing in worship.

Chapter 4

Worship in spirit and truth

In the first three chapters of the book I have raised a number of questions about corporate worship in the evangelical church: *What is the purpose of worship? Does singing have a valid role in worship? Are we doing more harm than good by singing? Is it really true that the music has no meaning, and therefore the choice of musical style is simply a matter of personal preference?*

I have also expressed concern about the issues of distraction and truthfulness in worship. Also, agreeing with the early Church Fathers, I have given prominence to the idea that corporate worship should symbolically represent—before God and, perhaps, before the angels of heaven—the unity of the Church, the body of Christ that includes all believers, past, present, and future. To be an adequate representation it was suggested that the unity within a worship service must extend beyond the mere gathering together of believers, beyond even their oneness in corporate recitation or song. It should include agreement in thought and emotion, to as great a degree as possible.

Finally, I have urged that within each individual there be a consistency of word, thought, and emotion, that worshipers not mindlessly recite a text, nor speak with a zeal that does not reflect their true feelings about the text.

In response to these chapters, one might be inclined to ask: *Where are all these questions and concerns coming from? Are they just the product of someone's imagination about some ideal worship? Worse yet, do they represent an attempt to impose some arbitrary requirements on worship in order to invalidate some particular forms of worship?*

In this chapter I will lay out what I believe to be a biblical foundation for worship that will provide answers to many of these questions, and others as well. Questions about singing in worship will, however, also require an understanding of congregational singing and of certain musical concepts. That will be the task of the chapters following this one.

A theoretical foundation for worship

Many people have observed that the New Testament contains very little information regarding worship. One passage that offers a succinct presentation of two basic requirements of worship is John 4:22–24. Recall the conversation between Jesus and the Samaritan woman at Jacob's well in Samaria. Their conversation quickly turned when she asked about the proper place for worship. This is Jesus's answer:

> You worship that which you do not know; we worship that which we know; for salvation is from the Jews. But an hour is coming, and now is, when the true worshipers shall worship the Father in spirit and truth; for such people the Father seeks to be His worshipers. God is spirit; and those who worship Him must worship in spirit and truth.
>
> (New American Standard Bible, 1973)

This passage is the biblical basis for the view of worship that underlies the discussions and conclusions of this book.

The Greek word used for "worship" in the above passage means "to fall down before another as an act of respect." When the one before whom a person bowed was clearly a superior being, perhaps supernatural or an earthly monarch, the act of falling down conveyed reverence and honor, and the implied intent to obey. This word occurs with this meaning many times in the Greek translation of the Old Testament (for example, in Genesis 18:2, 23:7; Numbers 22:31; and, 2 Samuel 9:6). In the New Testament the use of the word is restricted almost entirely to the worship of God and of His Son.

In this book I use the word *worship* to mean the following:

Definition: *Worship is the conscious, immediate, and appropriate response to God as a result of contemplation of the person and/or work of God as He has revealed Himself.*

I maintain that this definition preserves the meaning of "worship" to be our reverent, humble response when we become aware that we are in the presence of God. That presence is not perceived by physical sight but by the eye of faith as we are led to vistas of His glory, the result of contemplating His person and His work.

Also, according to this definition, worship originates with the individual, the member of the congregation, who is confronted with the glory of God. Thus worship is directed to God, not to the congregation.

Further, this definition requires that the one who would worship must first be led to reflect upon the glory of God. It is not enough to be taught the intricacies of church doctrine on topics such as baptism or the end-times. Nor does Bible teaching necessarily move us to reflect on God's glory. If the subject of the teaching is the person and/or work of God, then it is fine for worship, but any other teaching—such as helping people to understand a specific verse—is not appropriate to worship. It may, however, be very well-suited for an educational hour.

Worship is a time for believers to be refreshed in their knowledge of the glory of God. Their response might be a silent, moment-by-moment expression of thanksgiving or a plea for God's help to trust Him and lean upon His promised faithfulness, etc.

Now we formulate the definition of *corporate worship* that is at the heart of this book. It is intuitively clear that "corporate" worship does not occur just because two—or two thousand—people gather in one place to "worship." Suppose, for example, that a large group of believers assembles in one room and each engages in a time of personal, silent contemplation of the glory of God, with no connection to what each of the others is doing. Would that qualify as corporate worship? Surely not. The key phrase in this hypothetical situation is, of course, "with no connection to."

The early church helps us to define *corporate worship* by showing us that the many worshipers must speak with one voice. That is to say, the worship of the many must be unified—and that means far more than mere outward agreement, as in reciting a text. Instead corporate worship requires that when the worshipers read (or sing), they are unified in word, thought, and emotion, to as great a degree as possible.

Definition: *Corporate worship is the unified worship of two or more people.*

It follows from this definition that when people are gathered together for corporate worship and they have been jointly led to contemplate some aspect of God's glory, there should be a unified response that both agrees with the subject of the reflection and expresses an emotion appropriate to it.

Thus, time must be allocated for a response by the entire congregation. It is very interesting to observe that in churches where the sermon is viewed as Bible teaching—where little effort is made to lead people to the contemplation of God's glory—it is not unusual for the sermon, and even the service itself, to end rather abruptly, without providing an opportunity for congregational response. Instead, it's as though the lecture has ended, the bell has rung, and it's time to move on to the next class. This is most unfortunate.

Brief responses, like "Amen!" or "Thanks be to God!" and slightly longer ones, such as the *Gloria Patri* or *Doxology*, are appropriate and familiar enough that no printed text is necessary. When a more extensive response is called for (after the sermon, for instance), that response must have been prepared in advance and made available to the congregation in print or on a screen. If a song has a suitable text and music that supports that text, then by singing it, the congregation would probably be more unified than they would if only reading it aloud. If no such song is known, then the congregation could read a well-written text suitable to the subject of the contemplation.

In addition to these definitions of *worship* and *corporate worship*, the foundation for worship consists of four principles that are rooted in my interpretation of John 4:24. I will list these principles together with some conclusions that are important in the discussion of the music of congregational singing.

The first principle captures what, I believe, Jesus meant when He required that worship be "in spirit."

Principle I: *Worship in spirit is a new kind of worship in which one's response to the contemplation of God is communicated to God spiritually, through the inner spirit-being that is in union with Him.*

This principle requires that the one who would worship God in spirit must be born of the Spirit (recall Jesus's discussion with Nicodemus in John 3). Further, *worship in spirit* means that all of the worshiper's words, thoughts, and emotion are a part of his/her communication with God. This perspective is very different from "worship" that merely requires the completion of certain tasks.

The perspective that worship in spirit consists not merely of spoken words but includes the thoughts and emotion of the worshiper, takes on added import when we face the fact that our worship is not only to be in spirit but also truth. I will come back to this in the discussion following the statement of Principle III.

Principle II: *The content of worship must be the truth of God as revealed in the Scriptures.*

This means that the declarations in worship must be in line with God's revealed truth. There is no exception here for the texts of congregational songs. In contradiction to this, a double standard seems to exist in the church: error from the pulpit will not be tolerated, but error in a song is often met with, "Com' on, why the fuss? It's only a song!"

One way in which error creeps into song texts has already been mentioned; the author of the text lacks theological depth. This issue did not originate with contemporary Christian music, but in recent years it has become particularly acute in that arena. The problem is that many, probably most, contemporary song texts have been written by people whose background and training are in music, not theology.

Another error occurs when a scriptural text is distorted by the music it is set to. One example is the very popular setting of Matthew 6:33, *Seek Ye First*, composed in the early 1970s by Karen Lafferty. The tune gives to the text a sentimental tone, a sense that all will be "peaches and cream" if one simply seeks first the kingdom of God. This interpretation is far from biblical truth and far from the experience of a sizeable number of Christian martyrs, missionaries, and many others who have experienced great hardship as a result of giving the kingdom of God first place in their lives.

Note that *Seek Ye First* is another example in which the music does not really fit the text. In singing "O Sacred Head" to Webb the mismatch was obvious, but in the present example it is much less obvious. For this reason, it is to be feared that a person listening to the song frequently will, over time, tend to adopt an inaccurate understanding of the biblical text.

Another conclusion from Principle II is that the proclamation of truth calls for the proclamation of the fullness of truth. In Chapter 1, it was noted that in the nineteenth and early twentieth centuries, much of the evangelical church was focused on a narrow collection of topics—salvation, revival, the second coming of Christ, etc. The emphasis on these, however, meant that other important concepts in the truth of God were given insufficient attention.

Consider the 1905 gospel song, *I'm Only a Sinner, Saved by Grace*, written by James M. Gray (1851–1935), an educated pastor, and leader in the Bible Institute movement. The song became very popular among a large segment of the evangelical church. But ponder the statement, "I'm only a sinner ..." Where in those words is the perspective of imputed righteousness and a forgiven sinner's adoption into the family of God?

Emphasis on a narrow part of revealed truth inevitably produces a distortion of that truth. So, it is necessary that, over time, the worship of God should cover the broad spectrum of revealed truth. Therefore, the collection of texts readily available to the congregation for response by way of recitation or singing should span the range of God's truth.

This is reason enough to reject the practice of singing only the Psalms and a few other passages of Scripture ("exclusive psalmody"). But at the same time it would be folly to ignore the ancient as well as modern fears that the admission of "hymns of human composure" opens the door to false theology.

Similarly—but frequently overlooked—is the fact that error can occur easily in the case of exclusive psalmody. There are several ways in which this can happen, but the one of primary interest in this book is the influence of the music on the interpretation of the text.

Finally, revealed truth includes the unity of the Church across the world and throughout the ages. The Bible's emphasis on the oneness of the body of Christ speaks to the importance of the symbolic representation of unity in the worship service. For, if the worship service manifests disunity, then verbal proclamations of unity will ring hollow in the people's minds.

The third principle addresses the attitude of the worshiper.

Principle III: *Worship must be truthful.*

For worship to be "truthful" means that the worshipers must have good reason to believe that their communication to God is true. It is entirely possible that something is said (or sung) that is understood and believed, but is theologically incorrect. In this case, Principle III is satisfied because the worshipers have reason to believe that their expression is true, but Principle II is not sat-isfied, since their statement is actually false. This happens time and time again when the subject is one on which knowledgeable believers disagree.

Truthfulness in worship is more demanding than we might realize at first glance. Consider, for instance, just the case of con-gregational singing. How could a person sing dishonestly? One way is by singing the words mindlessly. Why is this a violation of truthfulness? Recall from Principle I that worship in spirit means that our words, thoughts, and emotions are all included in our com-munication to God. If we sing mindlessly, then our thoughts and, especially, our emotions are probably unrelated to the words that we sing, making it very likely that our full communication is not truthful.

Dishonest singing can also happen when the singer is dis-tracted by something, or is paying good attention to the text but not understanding it. For a long time, congregational expression in many churches has tended toward rapid, rote recitation (or sing-ing), as though the leaders are saying, "We have to do this, but let's get it over with quickly." In formal churches the tendency is to race through the recitation of creeds or the "Lord's Prayer." Also, congregational songs are often sung much too rapidly to allow the worshipers time even to "get the words out," let alone think about the text. The fault generally lies with the leadership, perhaps accompanists, who, consciously or not, set too fast a tempo.

Dishonesty also results when the text speaks of personal expe-rience that is not really true for most worshipers. The text might, for instance, express a depth of commitment that is so lofty as to be beyond the experience of most Christians. Texts written by the esteemed English hymn-writer, Charles Wesley (1707–1788), must be handled carefully for this very reason. Even a text that is considered one of his finest—"Jesus, Lover of My Soul"—must be used with great caution in a worship service because it gives voice to personal experience that is beyond that of a great many Christians.

A text might speak of waywardness that is true for some, but not for many others. It is quite shocking to hear mature Christians sing "Prone to wander, Lord I feel it, prone to leave the God I love." It is interesting to hear singers of those words respond to the question, "When was the last time you felt inclined to turn away from the faith?" Almost always the answer amounts to, "Well, never! But it's just a song."

A less obvious example of dishonesty is the case when the emotions that come with singing a text don't match what the singer really thinks about the text. A few years ago I was in a distant city on a Sunday, and attended an evening service in what was clearly a fine evangelical church. The congregation was made up largely of retired people, and, not surprisingly, the songs were drawn entirely from the gospel songs that they knew and loved.

The singing was accompanied by a skillful pianist who had obviously been mentored in the middle of the twentieth century when *evangelistic style accompaniment* was highly regarded. He used melodic and harmonic devices that are well-known to elicit strong emotional arousal. Even though I was very familiar with the devices and their emotional power, I found that I could not sing the texts honestly because the emotion stirred up by the accompaniment did not match my thinking about the texts. At the same time I found it impossible to ignore the music. It came as quite a surprise to realize that the only way for me to maintain integrity as I worshiped, was to stop singing.

This brings us to yet another challenge to truthfulness, one which is much deeper than those already mentioned. As we saw in Chapter 2, it is known that a positive emotional impulse, even one which is perceived only sub-consciously, can affect a person's thinking. This puts the serious worshiper, the person who desires to worship in spirit and truth, in a very difficult situation.

Suppose, for example, that the text of a congregational song leads a worshiper to profess a profound commitment to God. Usually, the music of the song is chosen to encourage a positive emotional response that can too easily lead the person to believe that the strong statement is true of himself/herself. In the moment, the worshiper appears to be making a truthful statement, but when the emotion subsides, the worshiper might realize that the text claims too much by way of commitment.

In the face of this subtle, but powerful, effect on one's thinking, what defense is available? First the church leadership should be sensitive to the problem when they choose the songs for worship. Since this is not often the case, the individual worshiper should learn to recognize the ways in which music arouses the emotions. This is not hard to do, even for those who have little or no background in music. In Chapters 5 and 6, as well as in *Worship and Congregational Singing,* I discuss some of the most common techniques used by composers.

The great effectiveness of these techniques has been demonstrated through centuries of Western music, and their success makes them also prime targets for abuse. That which gifted composers use to bring to music its great charm and power to stir its listeners, becomes in the hands of less-gifted writers mere tools by which to elevate the emotions through massive, careless overuse. This overuse was exactly what was on display in the piano accompaniment during that evening service I attended. Naturally, the congregation loved it, because we all enjoy an emotional arousal. However, truthfulness in worship may thereby be compromised without our being aware of it. If we learn to listen for the sound of these techniques, we will find it quite easy to recognize an effort to manipulate the listeners. Once identified, the effort can be rendered ineffective, but I know of no way to do so other than to stop singing.

A final concern about truthfulness in singing in worship is one that I have already mentioned more than once: *Can we truthfully sing a song with an emotion that is coming not from our reflection on the text but from the music?* Since the music is expected to enhance our emotional experience, the essential question here is whether it is even possible to sing in worship and remain truthful.

The fourth principle deals with another facet of truth. It is not explicitly found in John 4:24, but it follows from Principle II.

Principle IV: *The church should meet frequently for the purpose of corporate worship.*

Note that nothing is said here about a specific frequency or regular time of worship.

The unified worship of the church represents the true unity of the body of Christ more fully than any other corporate activity can. A watching world perceives that symbol only dimly, but the worshipers see it more clearly, and God Himself supremely so.

Unless there is frequent corporate worship our awareness of our oneness in Christ will fade and that unity can become just another point of doctrine that we believe rather than live.

Summary

This completes the brief survey of the foundation on which rests the view of worship presented in this book. For the sake of easy reference, I will list the definitions and principles presented in this chapter on a single page. After that we will turn to the task of understanding the music of congregational songs.

Definition: *Worship is the conscious, immediate, and appropriate response to God as a result of contemplation of the person and/or work of God as He has revealed Himself.*

Definition: *Corporate worship is the unified worship of two or more people.*

Principle I: *Worship in spirit is a new kind of worship in which one's response to the contemplation of God is communicated to God spiritually, through the inner spirit-being that is in union with Him.*

Principle II: *The content of worship must be the truth of God as revealed in the Scriptures.*

Principle III: *Worship must be truthful.*

Principle IV: *The church should meet frequently for the purpose of corporate worship.*

Chapter 5

From music to emotion

Two very important aspects of congregational song that I have mentioned from time to time in the previous chapters are the emotion that singing arouses in the worshiper, and the nagging possibility that, perhaps, meaning *can* be conveyed by the music itself. In our quest for a better understanding of congregational singing we must now turn to these issues.

In this chapter and the next I will offer a very brief account of how it is that music induces emotion in the listener. Some interesting and important results from scholarly research on emotion over the past three decades will be introduced. In Chapters 7 and 8 we will delve into the question of meaning in music.

Musical style

These discussions will involve the idea of a "musical style." Like many other concepts that we encounter in everyday life, there seems to be pretty good "intuitive" agreement about what is meant by "style of music." That is, when listening to music, most people would come up with—at least in general categories—the same answer when identifying its "style." Not many will listen to a Mozart symphony and identify its style as jazz, or country.

So, the idea of "musical style" is not foreign to us, but defining it is no easy task. In keeping with the promise to maintain a "bird's-eye view," I will be content with the intuitive sense that seems to be widely shared.

Expectation

It is important to the discussion of emotion induced by music to recognize that within the totality of the music written in a given style, there are certain patterns that turn up in many different places.

Consider, for example, the last phrase of the hymn tune Old Hundredth, composed by the French composer Louis Bourgeois (c.1510–1561)), shown in Figure 1. It is used most commonly for the familiar *Doxology,* whose text was written by Thomas Ken (1637–1711). (You are reminded that you can hear all of the figures in this book at www.neusong.com.)

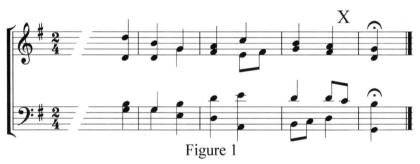

Figure 1

Suppose that you're familiar with traditional Western songs and that you happened to hear this music on the radio, never having heard it before. Even though the piece is completely new to you, when the music reaches the point marked by X in Figure 1, you would have a very strong sense of what the next chord is going to be. In fact, just the progression of the three chords right before X would be enough to give you that sense. In other words, something about the music up to and including X created in you a strong expectation of what was coming next.

Why? Because of your familiarity with the Western song style, you had heard a very similar short progression of chords many times in other compositions, and often the sequence ended in the same way. So, your mind—ever on the alert (not only when listening to music) to anticipate what is likely to happen next, in order to be better prepared to deal with it—put this outcome at the top of the list of possibilities.

This progression was so familiar to you because it is one of a number of patterns (known as "*cadences*") that composers use to bring pieces in this style, and many other styles, to a conclusion, or at least a temporary close.

Figure 2 shows another example, this one not involving a cadence. Try listening to just the first two chords on a piano, perhaps several times, and see if you have any idea of what might be coming next. Then listen to the entire progression in Figure 2. Does that sound like what you expected? Probably not. It doesn't sound badly out of place, but rarely does that pattern occur in traditional Western music.

The first two chords in Figure 3 are the same as those in Figure 2. Does the third chord sound like what you expected? Probably so. The second chord in Figures 2 and 3 is unique and so there are not many chords that "naturally" follow it.

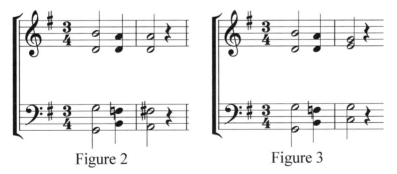

Figure 2   Figure 3

Where would you have heard such a progression? One example is almost any rendition of *Amazing Grace* by a secular performing artist. Almost always the harmony of the church version of the music is altered to something like that shown in Figure 4. There, in the second full measure (beginning at X), is the pattern of Figure 3.

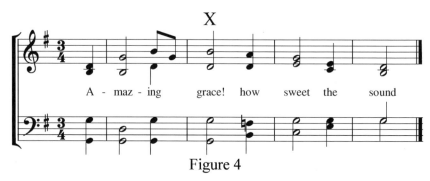

Figure 4

Now, listen to the church version (Figure 5). Do you get the same feeling in hearing the church version that you did when you heard the secular harmony?

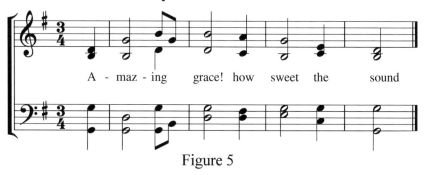

Figure 5

Here is another progression, beginning with the two chords in Figure 6. Do you have any expectation of what the next chord will

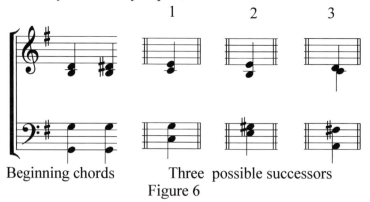

Beginning chords   Three possible successors

Figure 6

be? We offer three possibilities. Does any one of them sound like what you expected? How surprised would you be if one of the others was the one chosen by the composer to continue the pattern?

This progression using #1 as the successor seems most likely. It is found, for example, in the old chorus, *Thank You Lord for Saving My Soul*, and in other songs as well.

Figure 6 illustrates a type of pattern that is one of the most powerful emotion-inducing techniques. It is to use chords that contain "chromatic" tones. That is, tones that are not in the scale of the key in which the composition is written. Properly formed, the chords often sound lush. Like the second chord in Figure 2, chromatic chords tend to create strong expectations. Figure 7 shows part of

Figure 7

the Maori farewell song for which the evangelist and scholar J. Edwin Orr (1912–1987), supplied the Christian text, "Cleanse Me, O God" (also known as "Search Me, O God"). The music contains a number of chromatic chords. Can you hear the "lushness"?

Another way that composers use to generate expectations in listeners is by a succession of dissonant chords, that is, chords that might sound like the notes were chosen randomly, chords that clearly don't belong to the key in which the piece is written, or any other major or minor key. In the musical style of twentieth-century *art music,* dissonance is common, and a piece will often end on a dissonant chord.

But in classical and Romantic music of the eighteenth and nineteenth centuries it was almost obligatory that the composer bring the music back to a more normal, "consonant," sound before ending the piece. In other words, in those styles, a succession of dissonant chords established the expectation that the dissonance would end sooner or later.

When accompanying congregational singing an organist or pianist will sometimes "reharmonize" one verse. This sometimes brings in dissonant chords, but before the verse is over, consonance is once more established, bringing with it the fulfillment of everyone's expectation.

Many other examples can be given but we must move on to answer the pressing question: *What do expectations have to do with emotion induced by music?*

The role of expectations in inducing emotion

When an expectation is fulfilled, which is to say that one's expectation was correct, the mind produces a mild positive emotional impulse, something like what you get when you win a game of solitaire or complete a challenging crossword puzzle.

It turns out that the stronger the expectation, the greater the emotional impulse when the expectation becomes a reality. This is why you probably sensed a strong feeling when listening to *Amazing Grace* as in Figure 4. That strong feeling is undoubtedly the reason why this harmony is used so often in the secular versions of the song.

The musical techniques for generating powerful emotional impulses in listeners are known as "expressive effects." Chromaticism is one of them, but composers have found various other ways to increase the strength of the emotion that comes with fulfilled expectations. One common way—very popular in the baroque music of the seventeenth and eighteenth centuries and still effective today—is to delay the fulfillment of an expectation. The composer, however, has to be clever enough to keep the expectation alive.

The delay might be achieved by simply slowing down the music (a *ritard*) or by giving the listener the impression that fulfillment is at hand only to turn away for a moment before actually bringing fulfillment.

Figure 8

All of the great composers of traditional Western music have used these expressive effects in delightful ways to arouse emotion in listeners. Unfortunately, lesser composers, realizing the emotional effects of such methods, use them without the exquisite care that is necessary to preserve their beauty and unique power. Used without discretion they ultimately lose their sparkle and become just cheap means by which to manipulate people's emotions.

An interesting example is the well-known hymn tune St. Kevin, written by the English composer Sir Arthur S. Sullivan (1842–1900). It is often used with the text, "Come, Ye Faithful, Raise the Strain," written in the eighth century by St. John of Damascus, and translated by the eminent British hymnologist, John Mason Neale (1818–1866). Sullivan was best known for his light operas, composed in collaboration with Sir William Gilbert (1836–1911), who supplied the librettos.

In the nineteenth century it was quite common for composers to be rather undisciplined in their use of expressive effects, especially in light entertainment music, and in the music for gospel songs. One simple, and very popular expressive effect is shown in Figure 8. For listeners familiar with traditional Western music, the first chord establishes a fairly strong expectation that shortly one will hear the chord we have shown as the second chord in the progression.

What makes St. Kevin interesting is that within its four lines, Sullivan displays both tawdry, careless use of this expressive effect, and also an elegant use, one of the best to be found in all of hymnody. Figure 9 shows the inferior use, made so by tasteless repetition of essentially the same chord for a whole measure before satisfying the expectation at the start of the next measure.

Figure 9

Figure 10 shows the last line of St. Kevin, with the same chord at X. I'll skip a detailed analysis of why this is so beautiful an application of this expressive effect, but if you will listen to both Figure 9 and Figure 10 several times, you'll probably hear the difference.

Figure 10

One of the finest composers of all time, Johann Sebastian Bach (1685–1750), was masterful in his use of expressive effects. Figure 11 shows the closing measures of his setting of the German chorale (hymn) tune, Christ Ist Erstanden (Christ Has Risen). In

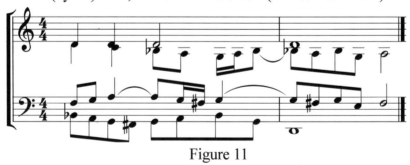

Figure 11

just these two measures alone, Bach uses dissonance, delay, one of those special chords that induces strong emotion, and even a bit of teasing that makes the listener feel like fulfillment is at hand only to move off for a moment before returning to the expected end. A thoughtful performer might add a *ritard* in the last measure even though none is indicated in the score.

An expectation is really just the mind's educated guess as to what might be coming next, or shortly, but composers will often surprise the listener by going a different way. An easy example is shown in Figures 12 and 13. Figure 12 shows the usual progression, ending as expected, but Figure 13 gives a frequent alternative ending that a composer might use if he/she intends the piece to continue on for a while.

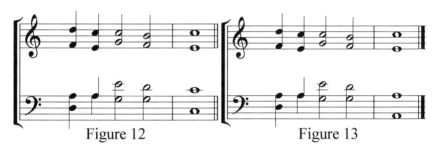

Figure 12   Figure 13

When an expectation is not fulfilled there might still be an emotional impulse, depending upon how the composer violates the expectation. Or the composer might allow that expectation to fade and replace it with new expectations as the music moves on.

In the next chapter we will see ways that music induces emotion in the listeners other than by expectations.

Chapter 6

Body, mind, and emotion

In Chapter 5, we saw one way in which music can prompt emotion in the listener: the composer creates and ultimately satisfies expectations. It is important to keep in mind that to be affected by this technique, the listener has no need of any musical training. All that is needed is familiarity with the style, passively gained through hours of listening to that style of music.

True, musical expertise enables individuals to develop a larger repertoire of expectations, thereby enhancing their enjoyment of a piece, but even the musically untutored easily acquire, without conscious effort, an astonishing collection of recognized patterns that give rise to expectations.

There are other ways by which music can stir the emotions of a listener. In this chapter we will look at several methods that are often used in contemporary secular and Christian music. This will require an understanding of how the body, mind, and emotions interact.

Another goal of this chapter is to deal, finally, with the question that has been raised several times: If we are to worship in spirit and truth, can we, with integrity, offer to the Lord the words of a song together with zeal that really isn't due to reflection on the text but rather to the music?

How can music arouse emotion?

Ultimately, our emotional response to music all comes down to our cognitive processing as we listen, but that statement is too general to be of much help. Here are three categories of cognitive processing that will help us understand how music prompts emotion.

First, some methods use the mind's innate emotion-producing techniques directly. As we've seen, one example is the positive impulse produced when an expectation is satisfied. (In the next chapter I will discuss associations in music that often induce emotion—a stirring march is an example.)

Like the use of expectations, another of these "direct" methods by which emotion is aroused is very familiar to us, but not often thought of in terms of music. The human mind has an "early-warning system" that responds very quickly (and sometimes inaccurately) when an in-coming stimulus is perceived as a threat to one's well-being.

While hiking in the woods one might hear a rustling in the leaves and immediately sense danger. A snake or some other wild animal might be present. Before the higher-level cognitive systems have a chance to evaluate the situation more carefully, we are already gearing up for action. Of course, the sound may have been entirely benign, in which case the mind sends out the "calm down" command, but—as we have all experienced—the emotional surge can take some time to subside.

What I just now described is an example of a fear response. It is likely to be invoked whenever we experience a sense of urgency. Loud music can trigger this reaction and thereby arouse the emotions (or, increase the intensity of an existing arousal). Indeed, a strong, positive relationship has been found between loudness and emotional arousal, meaning that the louder the music the stronger the emotion.

Interestingly, for several decades there has been a "loudness war" in the commercial popular music recording business, as producers have sought to overcome the CD's inherent limitations on loudness. Such is the thirst for emotional arousal.

A fast tempo, especially in conjunction with a certain degree of loudness, encourages a sense of urgency or tension. Again, the fear mechanism is triggered. We shall shortly see another way in which a fast tempo can induce emotion.

In the case of a fast tempo and the resulting emotional response, the important issue is the listener's *perception* of the tempo. The number of beats per minute might not tell the whole story. In evangelistic style playing, with all its "runs" up and down the keyboard, the tempo can seem faster than it really is. The same holds when the accompaniment consists of a strummed guitar.

Another way of musically activating the fear response is through surprise. This can be done by a very abrupt change of the key. One of the best known and most stirring examples in opera occurs in the "Grand March" from Verdi's (1813–1901) opera *Aida*. Since the 1950s this wonderful expressive device of abruptly changing the key has lost some of its charm through massive, careless overuse, especially in congregational singing.

Unexpected *syncopation*, as in the "Ode to Joy" section of Beethoven's (1770–1827) *Ninth Symphony*, is another way to surprise the listener. Syncopation has been a part of art music for centuries, but it did not "catch on" in the popular arena until the late nineteenth century with the ragtime music of Scott Joplin (1868–1917). Since then it has seen spectacular growth in music all over the world. Because of its overuse it has become the new "normal," and thereby lost some of its expressive freshness.

A third way to introduce surprise is by a beautiful violation of an expectation. A very simple example occurs when a hymn that is written in a minor key closes with an "Amen," but the last chord is major rather than the expected minor. The result can be stunningly

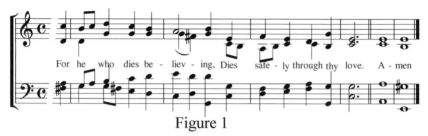

For he who dies be - liev - ing, Dies safe - ly through thy love. A - men

Figure 1

beautiful. A variant of this is found in Figure 1, which shows the last line of the Passion Chorale tune for "O Sacred Head," and an unexpected cadence for the "Amen."

This expressive effect has largely escaped the plague of over-use since rarely in recent centuries have congregational songs—especially gospel songs—been written in a minor key.

We must move on to other means by which emotion can be aroused through music. A second category is through memory. Many songs of the church carry with them highly emotional mem-ories, emotions that are experienced again every time that a song is sung. Probably the easiest examples to point to are the Christmas carols, but we can also include a song like *Just As I Am*, which has long been used to accompany an "invitation" at the end of a service, most notably in the evangelistic rallies of Billy Graham (b. 1918).

A final category of means by which music arouses the emo-tions is perhaps the most surprising, but for contemporary popular music, with its strong emphasis on rhythm, it is probably the most important.

For more than a century the very close relationship between emotion and the physical body has been recognized. When peo-ple experience emotion, changes occur in their heart rate, blood pressure, respiration rate, and skin conductance, as well as in their facial appearance, their body movements, and the sound of their voice.

Furthermore, there is evidence to suggest that in contexts where emotional arousal is a frequent occurrence (e.g., a rock concert or a worship service), artificially producing some of the physical symptoms of an arousal can lead the mind to construct a genuine emotional experience, or enhance an existing one.

For example, research shows that when a smiling person enters the room, others frequently begin to smile. This is an example of "mimicry," and it is something that we humans do sub-consciously, with great frequency, and lightning speed. The surprising thing is that when this happens, we actually tend to experience a degree of happiness! That is, from just one component, a smile, that usually accompanies the emotion of happiness, the mind creates the entire emotion, and the person tends to feel happy.

In fact, a relatively recent theory about empathy holds that when we observe the symptoms of another person's emotional experience, often through a facial expression, we automatically recreate that emotion within ourselves *and thereby are able to share his/her grief or joy, etc.* This happens in watching opera performances, motion pictures, or when observing expressive praise teams in contemporary worship.

But what does this have to do with emotion experienced when listening to music having emphatic, strong rhythm? In Western music we very quickly perceive the "beat." But much more than mere perception is taking place. One or more of the body's various muscle groups are "captured" by the beat and driven into the same frequency. We see this often when we observe a listener tapping a foot to the beat, or clapping the hands. Less easily observed is a change of respiration rate to match the beat, with associated change of heart rate.

Thus, there is physiological change, a major component of emotion, and, in the right contexts, the mind constructs an emotional experience that matches the physical changes. The process whereby a muscle group is driven by the beat is an example of *entrainment*, a concept that has been known for a long time in physics, but the recognition of its importance in music is more recent. It provides an interesting explanation for why "rhythm-centric" music stirs the emotions.

But there is more. When listening to music that has, say, a lot of repeated syncopation, people often begin to clap their hands or tap a foot, etc. But even if the visible motion is suppressed, it is known that such movement is still happening internally. That is, we might be in a setting where snapping the fingers or clapping the hands is not considered appropriate, and we can, by an act of the will, suppress the visible movement, but not the sense of movement in the mind.

By the mechanism of entrainment, a fast tempo can increase the heart and respiration rates even without the music's being loud. In suitable contexts, the mind can then create an emotional impulse.

Emotional impulses and the sub-conscious mind

It is an instructive exercise to watch a TV commercial and instead of giving attention to the content of what is being said (or sung), to try to notice what is going on in the background. For example, is there some music being played? What are the characteristics of the music? How are the actors dressed? Are there provocative elements that would escape conscious notice if the viewer's attention were focused on the product being touted?

Do the same for magazine advertisements, performances of vocal entertainers, and the conduct of church services.

What is the point of selectively focusing on elements that are "secondary"? This exercise helps us recognize a principle that has long been known and acted on in the advertising world. In recent decades this concept has become the focus of a great deal of study in the social sciences, especially social psychology.

What advertising has capitalized on is this: the secondary elements kept in the background (e.g., quiet music, subtle sexually-provocative attire) are chosen because they generally arouse positive emotions. The advertiser must handle these elements carefully, however, because if they become too prominent they will hijack the viewer's attention and take it away from the product itself. Even though the viewer's attention might not be drawn to those secondary elements, they are perceived sub-consciously.

The sub-conscious mind is aware of the impact of these "hidden" effects and attributes the resulting emotion to that which *is* the focus of attention, namely, the product being advertised. The usual result is just exactly what the advertiser was hoping for—the person looks upon the product more favorably, and is, therefore, more likely to buy it.

The technical term for this misidentification of the true source(s) of the emotion is "*misattribution*." A very large number and a wide variety of experiments have shown that the individual might or might not be aware of the arousal. In "real life" or in the laboratory, the idea is to "prime" the person with a certain feeling and then to assign a task of some sort to which the feeling will be transferred and applied (i.e., misattributed).

For example, the task in advertising is to create a positive evaluation of the product. The casual viewer has no idea of what has happened, but the sub-conscious positive feelings will likely have been misattributed to the product, creating the desired positive attitude toward it.

Or, if the task is to evaluate a proposed course of action, such as deciding to commit oneself to a certain career in Christian service, then the positive feeling that is prompted by quiet, emotion-arousing music, is easily transformed into a favorable view of the commitment, encouraging a positive decision.

Other interesting experiments have been done in which the participant is *subliminally* primed by a picture of either a frowning (or a smiling) person. Even though the participant has no recollection of seeing that picture, much less being able to identify it, the emotion represented by the face produces the same positive or negative feeling in the viewer. If the person is then asked to judge the truthfulness of a given statement, the emotion will likely be misattributed to yield a negative decision in the case of the frowning face, or a positive one if the "unseen" face was smiling.

Misattribution is likely to occur if the person was never aware of the arousal, or if the true source of the emotion was hidden, or if the assigned task takes the attention away from the true source of the emotion. For the purposes of this discussion, the most important point regarding misattribution of emotion is that since it all takes place in the sub-conscious mind, the individual is unaware that it has happened, and so, generally, has no reason to suspect that it has any effect on his/her response to the task.

An exception occurs when the result of the misattribution leads to a violation of something known to the individual. You probably experienced this in trying to sing "O Sacred Head" to the tune Webb. The march-like, triumphant Webb is not appropriate to a text having to do with the suffering of Christ: hence the attempted misattribution failed.

My experience in singing the gospel songs in the evening service (Chapter 4) was significantly different. While trying to attend to the text, the excessive emotion aroused by the accompaniment *was* misattributed to the text because the strong feeling seemed natural through years of experience in singing gospel songs. What interrupted the process was a diligent effort to interact with the text, which led to a realization that the emotion I felt was "over the top," amounting to a dishonest expression. I quickly turned my attention to the accompaniment and was convinced that the emotion was correctly attributed to it. But inattentiveness to the text while continuing to sing is a form of dishonesty, and is therefore unacceptable (Principle III). However, when I turned my attention back to the content of what I was singing, the attribution followed right with it, and the emotion was again misattributed to the text. The only way out of this dilemma was to stop singing, which damages unity, but seemed to be the lesser of two evils.

What made this different from the experience of trying to sing "O Sacred Head" to Webb is that the misfit in this latter case was so blatant, whereas in the former case, that of the gospel song, the unwary mind had grown accustomed to accepting the misattribution and "bending" the text to suit the feeling. In the case of Webb, that would be much too great a stretch.

Misattribution, the singer's friend

I have raised the question of whether it is even possible to sing in worship and be truthful. As I have said before, in singing we are presenting to the Lord a text with an emotional force that is not entirely due to our reflection on the meaning of that text, but rather finds significant strength in the music. It is as though we want the Lord to think that the zeal with which we sing represents our true feeling about the text. Can this be truthful when some of that zeal is really due to the music?

Suppose that the song being sung has an excellent text and that the worshiper is concentrating on it. Further, we assume that the music (including the accompaniment) adds a *modest* emotional impulse of a type that suits the text well. If these conditions are satisfied, then the mind will undoubtedly misattribute the emotional impulse to the text. But since the music is assumed to fit the text well and the emotional boost is not excessive, the singer will have no reason to challenge it.

In other words, in the mind of the singer, the emotional contribution of the music *is* due to his/her reflection on the text. Furthermore, the added emotional impulse overcomes the lack of zeal, the "coldness" that is an inherent problem in joint congregational expression (as was observed by Calvin). Thus, the worshiper is offering the text to the Lord with even greater integrity. Therefore, misattribution can help the singer to conform more closely to the truthfulness that Principle III requires in worship.

Chapter 7

Can music convey meaning?

Up to this point, the discussion of emotion induced by music has focused on its intensity. Does the music supply too strong an emotional boost for the given text? In the secular version of *Amazing Grace*, for instance, I claimed that there is a stronger emotional impulse than that supplied by the traditional version of the music used in church services. Arguably, the increased emotional force distorts the text in the mind of the singer.

A similar question arises in the hymn tune Toplady, composed by Thomas Hastings (1784–1872). It is the traditional tune for Augustus Toplady's (1740–1778) text "Rock of Ages," one of the

Figure 1

best-loved songs of the church for almost two centuries. In the second line, shown in Figure 1, we find repeated two times the same rather tasteless expressive device that I criticized in the second line of Sullivan's tune, St. Kevin (Chapter 5, Figure 9). It consists of a full measure of basically the same chord, emphasizing an expectation not fulfilled until the next measure. Evidently, the composer was trying to boost the emotional impulse that the singer feels when the expectation is finally satisfied.

The Toplady tune is not generally considered one of the better hymn tunes, and for years an effort was made to encourage the use of an alternate tune that would supply a less intense emotional impulse. But the effort was to no avail. Perhaps the failure to replace Toplady was due to the fact that "Rock of Ages" dwells on death and the subsequent judgment, topics that reach to the deepest part of the soul, and, as such, are well-served by the intensity of Toplady. By contrast, the proposed alternative (known as Redhead) sounds too "matter of fact" for this subject.

But emotional supplementation in singing is not only a matter of the strength of the added emotional impulse. For example, the criticism of Karen Lafferty's song, *Seek Ye First*, was not primarily that the supplied emotion was too intense. My concern is that the music conveys to the singer a sense that seeking first the kingdom of God is a blissful task, sure to yield a quiet, peaceful earthly life. This perspective conflicts with Jesus's own admonition and the experience of countless Christian believers through two millennia who have found that seeking first the kingdom of God is far from blissful. Moreover, the song makes no mention of the nature of "all these things," but the biblical context of this phrase speaks of the necessities of life, not smooth sailing on a quiet sea.

Or, think, yet again, on the suggestion that you sing "O Sacred Head" to the tune Webb. The emotional intensity of the music was not the problem. Instead, the music just doesn't "fit" the text. What does that mean? The music certainly matches the text in the number of syllables per line and the musical accent matches very well the accent in each word. So what is the problem? It is that Webb imparts a martial, triumphant, joyful sense that is far removed from the sorrowful, reflective nature of the text.

This raises one question for this chapter: *Can music itself connote sorrow, peace, exuberance, happiness, etc.?* That is, can music not only induce an emotion but specify a certain *type* of emotion (e.g., joy, sorrow, happiness, fear)? Or, when emotion results from a fulfilled expectation, as in Chapter 5, is this just an undifferentiated emotional impulse, a "raw" or generic emotion? If, instead, music can tag the emotion as sorrowful or triumphant, etc., how does it do this?

If we set aside any reference to emotion, we arrive at a more general—and, for present purposes, a more important—question: *Can music communicate meaning?*

Meaning in music

The latter part of the eighteenth century saw the rise of "pure" instrumental music, which is to say, music not composed to accompany a text, nor tied to an extramusical concept by title (e.g., Claude Debussy's (1862–1918), *Clair de lune* ("Moonlight")) or "program notes," (e.g., to accompany Modest Mussorgsky's (1839–1881), *Pictures at an Exhibition*) nor used in conjunction with another medium such as a drama or ballet. Examples include orchestral symphonies and concertos.

Since the listeners would have neither verbal nor visual image that would enable them to assign some external meaning to the music, the question arose: *Is it possible for such music to convey any external meaning?* For the better part of two centuries, the scholars who studied Western music became increasingly devoted to the principle that the only meaning in "pure" music was to be found exclusively within the music itself.

This view was famously summarized by the Austrian music critic Eduard Hanslick (1825–1904), who wrote, "Music's complete content and total subject matter is nothing other than tonal form in movement." In other words, the only meaning in "pure" music was to be found in its structure, its melodic, harmonic, and rhythmic intricacies, the variation in its themes, the way in which the instruments are used, etc. This perspective came to be known as the "absolutist" view.

Arguably, most leaders in the modern evangelical church are committed to the absolutist position. This is apparent from the frequently-used phrase, "The music makes no difference, only the words." Those of this persuasion argue that the music conveys no meaning in itself, and so the only source of meaning is the text. Yet, when asked to sing "O Sacred Head" to Webb, most of these same people would cringe at the "inappropriateness" of the music!

In his 1956 book, *Emotion and Meaning in Music*, the well-respected American *musicologist*, Leonard B. Meyer (1918–2007), took issue with the absolutist position.[1] "The musical theory and practice of many different cultures in many different epochs indicates that music can and does convey referential meaning," he wrote. By this he meant that music can "refer to the extramusical world of concepts, actions, emotional states, and character."

In the next chapter we will see that strong support for Meyer's "referential" view was found by ethnomusicologists working in a variety of cultures. In the late twentieth century, more and more musicologists were coming to Meyer's position. But, alas! The evangelical church clings to its absolutism as justification for the use of all manner of popular secular musical styles in worship.

Associations

When speaking of "referential meaning," we are talking about references to concepts, actions, etc., external to the music, references formed in the mind of the listener solely by the music itself (including instrumentation, characteristics of the performers, venue, etc.), rather than by any text or dramatic scene attached to the music.

These external references are also known as "extramusical references," or "associations," and by some as "musical gestures." I

1. Meyer, Leonard B. *Emotion and Meaning in Music*. Chicago: University of Chicago Press, 1956.

will speak primarily of "associations," but there is a great deal of help to be found in thinking of these references as "gestures." This is because they share many of the characteristics of the physical gestures which we effortlessly use in communicating with others.

Here are some of the more important similarities between musical associations and physical gestures. Just as physical gestures are highly culture-specific, so also musical associations are specific to a given musical style. Missionaries and business travelers to foreign cultures must be made aware of any of their physical gestures that could be interpreted very differently in their home culture and in the country they are visiting. So also, associations in one musical style might not exist in a different style, or, might have a different meaning. We will see examples in the next chapter.

In a very large percentage of cases, the physical gestures we use, or observe, in communication with others are never used, or perceived consciously. When a person becomes thoroughly familiar with a culture, that culture's gestures are instantly and effortlessly assimilated by the mind to add nuance to the spoken words. The same is true of associations in the music of songs. By familiarity with a given style, the associations are automatically understood at the sub-conscious level, and become an integral part of the meaning of the text.

Still another similarity between physical gestures and musical associations lies in the fact that rarely, if ever, are they "one-dimensional." For example, even within the narrow slice of Western culture that is found in the United States, a "simple" smile is an ambiguous gesture. It often connotes pleasure or delight, but if one has just made an offer on a used car, a smile by the owner might indicate disdain, as if to say "You can't be serious!" Any ambiguity is generally clarified by other physical characteristics, such as the position of the head, the "look" in the eye, accompanying hand gestures, or a host of contextual factors (like attire, and the nature of the activity). Musical associations also rely on a multiplicity of musical dimensions such as tempo, melody, harmony, rhythm, tonality (major or minor key), dynamics (loud/soft), choice of instruments, and mannerisms of the performer(s). Just as with a smile, it can be exceedingly difficult, well-nigh impossible, to ferret out all the accompanying features that go into making up the exact meaning, yet we understand that meaning with remarkable ease and accuracy.

We must make it clear that the associations of interest in this study, are those which are similarly understood by everyone who is familiar with a given musical style.

Finally, before we turn to a number of examples, we should consider the question of how musical associations come to be. One way is by virtue of the repeated use, over time, of a particular collection of musical characteristics in settings that share a common meaning. That meaning might originally have become known by texts that the music accompanied, or by virtue of the activity for which the music has been the traditional accompaniment (e.g., a visit by a reigning monarch). Sometimes the sound of the music, or its rhythmic structure, might even resemble in some way an event in the extramusical world.

Examples of associations

Here are several examples of associations that are found in a variety of musical styles in Western culture.

When we hear quiet music in a minor key, with a slow tempo, and using tones that are in the lower range, sorrow, perhaps associated with death, is apt to come to mind. This is a direct reflection of how we in Western culture react to death. In certain African cultures the attitude toward death, however, is very different: death is associated with "frenzied musical activity." This is a good example to show the multi-dimensionality of associations: it is not sufficient only that the music be in a minor key. The traditional music for the Christmas carol, *God Rest Ye Merry, Gentlemen*, is in a minor key, but the music certainly does not engender sorrow or thoughts of death.

An association that is found in much of the gospel song genre makes repeated use of a rhythmic pattern known as "skipping rhythm," or "dotted-eighth rhythm." Used in conjunction with a reasonably fast tempo, a major key, and a melody toward the higher range, it connotes happiness, lightheartedness, or gaiety. It reminds one of a child skipping down the sidewalk, hence the name.

Figure 2

Figure 2 shows an example of this in the melody that usually accompanies the old gospel song by Russell Kelso Carter (1849–1928), *Standing on the Promises*. Again, this association depends upon multiple musical dimensions. The skipping rhythm by itself is not sufficient, as is demonstrated by Chopin's (1810–1849) familiar *Funeral March*, the theme of which is shown in Figure 3. It is in a minor key and in a low range. When played slowly it does, indeed, sound like a funeral march.

Figure 3

When we hear a brass ensemble playing music in a major key, in 4/4 time, and with a modest tempo and notes mostly of equal duration, we easily think of a military march, hence confidence, determination, even victory. The traditional tune for *Onward, Christian Soldiers*, composed by Arthur Sullivan, is a good example. So also is the tune Sine Nomine, composed by the celebrated English composer Ralph Vaughan Williams (1872–1958). Its confident, victorious sense makes it an ideal accompaniment for Bishop William Walsham How's (1823–1897) text, "For All the Saints," which celebrates the final triumph of Christ and His host of faithful believers.

An association that is familiar in country music is a "catch" in the singer's voice, a very brief musical "ornament" consisting of a note or two in a high range. It is intended to suggest grief, as in the loss of a loved one.

A pattern found often in Irish and Scottish folk songs consists of a large ascending interval followed by two steps down the scale. It can connote longing or nostalgia, and so we have called it the "longing pattern."

Consider the example in Figure 4, which consists of one line from the music for the Scottish song, *My Bonnie Lies Over the Ocean*. The proposed longing pattern consists of the circled notes.

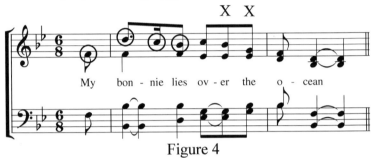

Figure 4

The sense of longing seems fairly strong. But in Figure 5 we show a part of the first line of Aurelia, the hymn tune composed by Samuel Sebastian Wesley (1810–1876), commonly used for Samuel Stone's (1839–1900) text, "The Church's One Foundation." The longing pattern (circled) appears here, but there is no trace of longing. What accounts for the difference between this and the feeling in *My Bonnie*?

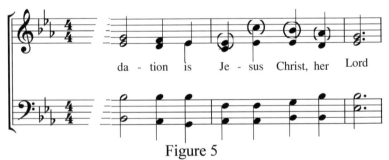

Figure 5

That question is usually very difficult to answer thoroughly. Music has so many dimensions, and within each dimension, such as tempo, there is a considerable range. Moreover, very slight differences can alter the meaning. One has only to consider the huge array of possibilities in a physical gesture to appreciate the subtlety of musical gestures (that is, associations).

Nevertheless, we should make an effort to find at least one or two factor(s) that help to explain the apparent absence of longing in Aurelia. A fruitful way to do this is to look at other examples of this pattern. For instance, whatever may have been the true source of the tune Londonderry Air (*O Danny Boy*), it does have the longing pattern, and the strong sense of longing is reinforced by the text attached to the pattern, "Tis I'll be here in sunshine ..." Another example is the Scottish song *Annie Laurie*. Again, the longing pattern is present, and the sense of longing is strong from the music as well as the text.

The classic American folk songs, *Home, Sweet Home* ("there's no place ...") and *Dixie* ("I wish I was in ...") are also examples of the longing pattern, although in the latter case the large ascending interval is split into two smaller ascending intervals. Near the beginning of the choruses of the old gospel song *God Be with You Til We Meet Again*, and the more recent and much loved *How Great Thou Art*, we find the pattern, again with the large ascending interval broken up into two smaller intervals. The sense of longing is quite strong in the music of both songs.

Incidentally, a similar pattern exists in *Amazing Grace* (Chapter 5, Figure 4). In that secular version the longing feeling is strong, but in the church version (Chapter 5, Figure 5) it is much reduced.

As a final example, *In Christ Alone*—the recent, and very popular song by Keith Getty (b. 1974) and Stuart Townend (b. 1963)—has the pattern ("when fears are stilled"); again, the longing feeling in the music is strong.

In these songs, are the contexts of the longing pattern similar in any way? Something that might give us a clue? Yes. In each case the pattern leads to a chord, marked by Xs in Figure 4, whose root is the fourth note of the scale (hence the chord is known as a IV chord). There is some basis for the argument that this chord is responsible for the strengthened sense of nostalgia. Significantly, this pattern is absent in Aurelia. In the church version of *Amazing Grace*, there is a IV chord, but its presence is very weak.

Thus, the presence of this chord seems to play a prominent role in the longing pattern, but have we accounted for all the components that make up this association? Undoubtedly the answer is, "No." But I know of no examples that suggest that there are others.

Consider a couple of examples that will be dear to the heart of any boy who grew up in mid-twentieth century America. A favorite radio program was *The Lone Ranger*, the fictitious exploits of a masked man who, with his horse, *Silver*, and his faithful companion, *Tonto*, helped to maintain law and order in the wild American west of the nineteenth century.

The familiar musical themes used in every episode were actually taken from the Overture to Gioachino Rossini's (1792–1868) *William Tell* opera. Rossini had no such idea in mind when he was composing, but one of the patterns in the music seems to help one visualize a galloping horse, and so those responsible for the program decided to use that part of the music of the Overture to accompany the Lone Ranger's riding to the rescue or pursuing a villain.

Another part of the music accompanied the Lone Ranger's riding off in victory, his work on that case completed. Interestingly, the longing pattern (followed by several IV chords) occurs prominently in that passage, encouraging in the young listeners a sentimental sense, to remember the many—always happy—conclusions of programs past.

In Chapter 5, we briefly mentioned chromaticism as a source of expectations, hence of emotion. It has also been used for centuries in Western art music to communicate meaning, particularly the extraordinary, such as an intense feeling, anguish, or misery. Musicologist Theo van Leeuwen asserts that chromaticism "is a standard device of 'sentimentality' in music," while musicologist Susan McClary sees it as representing "the irrational or deviant."

The precise meaning of chromaticism in a given piece depends, as usual, on other musical dimensions such as rhythm and tempo.

Van Leeuwen also argues that in Western music, large ascending intervals in the melody connote confidence and boldness. This sense is strengthened by a loud dynamic level and marching meter. There are many examples from the songs of the church: Lyons (*O Worship the King* (even though it is in triple meter)); Leoni (*The God of Abraham Praise*); Easter Hymn (*Christ the Lord Is Risen Today*); Coronation (*All Hail the Power of Jesus' Name!*); and, Sine Nomine (*For All the Saints*).

By contrast, intervals that are small (just a few half-steps) convey a sense of reflection and introspection. This sense is reinforced by triple meter, a soft sound, a relatively slow tempo, and, often, chromaticism. One of the finest examples is Hamburg, the tune almost always used in America for "When I Survey the Wondrous Cross." Even though it is in 4/4 time, the fact that each measure begins with a half-note gives the feeling of triple (3/4) time. The largest interval in the song is two half-steps, and the total range of the melody is unusually small, the equivalent of six half-steps. The slow tempo and small intervals fit well the meditative text.

In the current effort to compose contemporary-style tunes for old texts, a new setting for "For All the Saints" has been written. It is striking in its heavy use of the characteristics befitting contemplative texts, making it most unsatisfactory as the accompaniment for the triumphant "For All the Saints." This poor fit manifests the lingering absolutist view in the church that as long as the text is biblical, the music makes no difference.

What real difference do associations make in singing?

Even if—as many now believe—associations, or external references, do exist in music, is that fact any more than just an interesting bit of trivia? More specifically, do associations make any significant difference in congregational singing? Well, remember that the associations made a big difference when we tried to sing "O Sacred Head" to Webb, so we ought not to be too hasty in dismissing the whole idea that associations might have a strong impact in congregational singing.

What seems to throw people off-course and keep them from understanding this, is the fact that the meaning conveyed by text is of a very different form from that communicated by music. By its very nature, a text cannot be understood unless one's attention is fixed on it, but the external references that are suggested by music are almost always perceived sub-consciously, and automatically. When singing "O Worship the King" to the tune Lyons, no one thinks about the large ascending intervals and concludes that the composer intended to communicate boldness and confidence. The tune simply instills in us that sense.

This difference between how text and music communicate has a very significant consequence. Because most associations are perceived sub-consciously, they seem to come from within and so are not questioned. But the meaning conveyed by text requires our attention; it is open to reflection and challenge, or can be ignored even if we continue to sing the words. In more direct terms, we can ignore the meaning of the text, but not that of the music. This is one reason, among others, that music can be *very* powerful, quite apart from its emotional impact.

Associations in the music interact with the text in much the same way that emotion does. There are three possibilities if one is giving attention to the text. First, if the meaning communicated by the music is not at all suited to that of the text, as in the case of "O Sacred Head" and Webb, then singers will find it very difficult to concentrate on the text. If so inclined, they might try to understand what has caused the problem, but, more likely, their minds will just drift away from worship to something else.

Second, the meaning conveyed by the music might exquisitely supplement the text and will be readily incorporated into the singers's response, which is to say, into their worship. Of course, this is the ideal situation—and I believe this to be the only legitimate justification for singing in worship.

In the third situation that can arise, some modification of the meaning of the text (i.e., "bending" the text) will cause the meaning of the music to seem suitable. A serious problem in this case occurs when the changed perspective on the text results in a meaning contrary to biblical truth. This happens more often than one might think. Using, for instance, the music of a popular love song, or music reminiscent of a love song, for a text about the love of God, or a person's love for God, will undoubtedly distort the true love of God. Similarly, quoting Psalm 51 with the lighthearted syncopation of the anonymous song, *Create in Me a Clean Heart*, cannot but trivialize the enormous gravity of the verse, "Take not Thy Holy Spirit from me." And, we have already mentioned the unfortunate sentimentality that arises from Karen Lafferty's setting of *Seek Ye First*.

In all of this discussion about meaning in music, our primary concern is the fact that, through the associations, *the music acts as a commentary on the text*, for good or ill. In the next chapters we will see the profound effect this misunderstanding has had—and continues to have—on a largely-unsuspecting church.

Chapter 8

Music, a powerful persuader

Have you ever wondered why the counter-culture movement of the 1960s didn't set their lyrics to, say, lullaby tunes? Doing so would surely have made their music—and perhaps their ideas, as well—more readily acceptable to the general public.

Had you been in charge of the Civil Rights Movement in the 1960s, would you have suggested that instead of the quiet, reflective *We Shall Overcome,* they use as their theme song the stirring music of *Onward, Christian Soldiers*—and perhaps some of the text as well? Wouldn't that choice have done a better job of rallying the troops?

Clearly, the leaders of both these movements had something deeper in mind. After all, these were people with a cause. They weren't using the music merely as an identifying mark; they regarded music as a means of conveying significant characteristics of their cause.

In their study of music's functions in societies, ethnomusicologists have isolated several widespread uses. We have already briefly discussed emotional expression (Chapter 6), and communication (Chapter 7). The focus of this chapter is the very important rhetorical function of music: its use in persuasion.

We have already seen one way in which music acts as a persuader. When music stirs positive emotions, it affects people's judgment, making it more likely that they will, for instance, believe a statement to be true, or will think more positively about a given product, etc. The music here only serves to arouse the emotions. The same results have been achieved with subliminal methods without any reference to, or use of, music.

The persuasiveness of music goes well beyond its ability to stir the emotions and thereby influence and perhaps even prompt actions. By means of associations music can bring to a person's mind external concepts, attitudes, and actions, even if only subconsciously. In this chapter we will get a glimpse of the far-reaching implications of this capability.

Groups

Since associations, like gestures, are culture-specific, let us assume that for the purposes of this chapter we have the Western culture in mind. We will also assume that the Western culture's prominent musical styles are so widely heard and/or seen that just about everyone is familiar with the basic associations in the various styles.

By no means are we assuming that everyone *likes* this style or that, but just that everyone grasps the meaning of each style's more common associations. To be sure, more subtle associations of one style or another might not be recognized without more concentrated exposure to it.

Within any large culture there are collections of people who are bound together by some particular perspectives, attitudes or goals. Researchers call such a collection a "group," and those shared concepts that bind them together are called "values."

When speaking of group values, we aren't necessarily referring to moral or ethical values. Group values are simply the tenets that give the group cohesion. The central values—the ones most important to the group—are called "core" values. A few examples will clarify these ideas.

The counter-culture of the 1960s was a group of (mostly younger) adults who were devoted to the rejection of authority, to the defiance of traditional cultural norms, and, in general, to a hedonistic lifestyle. These were core values for the group.

The Civil Rights Movement was a group of primarily African-Americans who were committed to freedom, equality, justice, and non-violence. These were core values.

Another group of interest is the "Protestant" group, which can be divided into "subgroups" in a variety of ways: by, for instance, theological perspective (Calvinist, Wesleyan, Lutheran, etc.); eschatological persuasion (amillennial, post-millennial, pre-millennial); style of worship (highly formal, somewhat formal, very informal); musical preference (classic hymn, gospel song, contemporary praise music); and denomination, etc. While the various subgroups have many values in common, there are distinctive core values that separate them from one another.

In many cases, especially among groups which are strongly devoted to their core values, one finds that the group adopts, or espouses, a musical style that seems appropriate to its value-system. The group modifies an existing style to include associations that express its core values. As we will see in the rest of this chapter, the music espoused by a group is a very powerful, yet rarely acknowledged, agent of persuasion for its core values.

For example, in Chapter 1, I referred to the populist group of evangelicals in the early nineteenth century, who were devoted to revivalism, theological simplicity, and emotional intensity. They gave special attention to salvation and the second coming of Christ. The classic hymn form was seen as much too sober to support their devotion to these values. In particular, it lacked adequate emotion-inducing power. And so, over a period of several decades they forged a new style of music, enhancing the classic hymn form with elements of the campmeeting songs (which constituted the group music of evangelicalism on the American frontier in the early nineteenth century). In the latter part of the nineteenth century this new style soared in popularity throughout America as a result of the Moody/Sankey revival meetings. It is now known as the gospel song genre. In the first half of the twentieth century it was the group music of the segment of evangelicalism that maintained, in a somewhat muted fashion, the values of revivalism, theological simplicity, emotional intensity, etc.

Similarly, the leaders of the Civil Rights Movement developed a style that used existing musical forms that were associated with a quiet confidence that expressed their core value of non-violence. (We will shortly see several quotations that speak to the effectiveness of their music.)

The strong anti-authoritarianism and aggressive defiance of traditional norms that characterized the 1960s cultural revolution, were well represented in the associations rooted in hard rock. Even those people who were strongly opposed to the core values of the group easily grasped those values in their music.

Our understanding of the importance of a group's music is aided by two propositions supported with evidence from scholarly sources.

Proposition I

The first proposition is quite straightforward: *The core values of a group are supported by the music it espouses.*

The assertion that the music "*supports*" a value means that the music facilitates in the listeners a positive perspective on the value. In addition to the three examples cited above, here are several more—of many that could be cited—from scholars and other notable people.

• Just after the end of World War I, the noted American composer Charles Wakefield Cadman (1881–1946), described jazz as "an exotic expression of our present national life. ... Its very rhythms and its fantastic effects ... somehow reflect the restless energy that pulses through the 'spirit of the day,' a restlessness that has become most patent since the World War."

• In 1954, the ethnomusicologist David McAllester (1916–2006), published the results of his study of Navajo music, research he described as "an attempt to explore cultural values through an analysis of attitudes toward music and through an analysis of the music itself." McAllester was clearly convinced that group music is a reliable reflection of that group's values.

• Another ethnomusicologist, Alan Lomax (1915–2002), studied the folk music of various societies. One very interesting result was his discovery that the organization of group singing often reflected the society's social organization. For example, when monophonic music (e.g., unison singing) was predominant, the society tended to be "leaderless": consensus and conformity described the methods of their social organization.

• David J. Elliott is a professional musician and scholar especially interested in music education. In 1995, he wrote: Creating and performing music "are powerful ways of capturing and delineating the character of a culture." He went on to suggest what I believe to be a very perceptive insight: our liking or disliking of a musical piece might be attributable to how well the cultural values perceived in the music (including the performance characteristics) match our own cultural beliefs and values.

• Theodore Gracyk is a philosopher and academician with professional interest in the philosophy of music. Writing in defense of rock music, he included this parenthetical comment, "The use of an eighth-note pulse in the guitar and bass was one of the mainstays of punk and new wave, creating a good deal of its propulsion and thus aggression." He apparently associated the "eighth-note pulse in the guitar and bass" with aggression, a core value of the devotees of punk rock.

• Philip Tagg (b. 1944) is a British musicologist who has specialized in popular music and has done a great deal of work on meaning in music. He maintains the existence of a well-established association in heavy metal music between strong electric guitar distortion and powerful motorcycles, like Harleys. Such distortion easily becomes associated with motorcycle gangs, and in another step, the association extends to their stereotypical values of rebellion, freedom, etc.

Tagg also claims that the music for film and television confirms a long-standing association between sex and the saxophone when it is played in a slightly jazzy, legato style. This was very much in evidence in the first half of the twentieth century when a large American sub-culture had liberation from traditional sexual mores as a core value. Its chosen music was jazz and the principal instrument was the saxophone.

• An especially interesting example comes from the work of the anthropologist, ethnomusicologist, and jazz musician Ernest Borneman (1915–1995). Consider his observation of African music in relation to values of African culture:

> While the whole European tradition strives for regularity—of pitch, of time, of timbre and of vibrato —the African tradition strives precisely for the negation of these elements. In language, the African tradition aims at circumlocution rather than at exact definition. The direct statement is considered crude and unimaginative; the veiling of all contents in ever-changing paraphrases is considered the criterion of intelligence and personality. In music, the same tendency towards obliquity and ellipsis is noticeable: no note is attacked straight; the voice or instrument always approaches it from above or below, plays around the implied pitch without ever remaining on it for any length of time, and departs from it without ever having committed itself to a single meaning. The timbre is veiled and paraphrased by constantly changing vibrato, tremolo and overtone effects. The timing and accentuation, finally, are not stated, but implied or suggested. The musician challenges himself to find and hold his orientation while denying or withholding all signposts.

• A final example in support of Proposition I comes from the work of the British ethnomusicologist John Blacking (1928–1990).

Regarding the movement against apartheid in South Africa, Blacking wrote this:

> The effectiveness of the South African Freedom Songs has been discussed chiefly in terms of their words, but it was their music which made the deepest impact, especially on those who did not speak the language in which the sentiments of the songs were expressed. The combination of the triads and cadences of European hymn-tunes and the rhythms and parallel movement of traditional African music expressed the new solidarity and values of urban groups: the sound of the music conveyed as clear a message as the words of the songs."

Proposition II

Proposition I affirms the communication of a group's core values through its music. Proposition II addresses the effects of group music on those who listen to it regularly. It asserts: *The values supported by a musical style tend to be adopted by, or reinforced in, those who are avid listeners of it.*

"Adopting a value" means that one's attitude and behavior become habitually influenced by that value. This does *not* mean necessarily that the individuals consciously perceive the value nor that they intentionally decide to embrace it.

Thus, for members of a group, the music of the group serves to reinforce its core values, at least sub-consciously. Some people who are not group members but who are avid listeners of its music (perhaps finding it very enjoyable) will, over time, tend to adopt the group's values, either intentionally or sub-consciously. Note that Proposition II gives no indication of how long it might take for an avid listener to be significantly influenced by a value. Undoubtedly that "adoption time" is subject to a variety of individual factors, two likely ones being the age of the listener and how staunchly he/she has been committed to an opposing value.

Again, there are countless examples that could be cited, but space prohibits mentioning more than these few:

• In his celebrated *Republic*, the ancient Greek philosopher/ mathematician Plato (~428 BC–347 BC) expressed the view that "when the modes of music change, the fundamental laws of the State always change with them."

• The Hellenistic Jewish philosopher Philo (~20 BC–AD ~50), wrote about the annual Jewish Day of Atonement. Ridiculed by the Greeks as the "Feast of Fasting," the celebration was mocked by many adherents to false religions because it lacked the revelry that they associated with their pagan feasts. Their feasts typically included "bantering and merry-making to the accompaniment of flutes and citharas, the sound of drums and cymbals and other effeminate and frivolous music of every kind, enkindling unbridled lusts with the help of the sense of hearing."

• The fourteenth-century Pope John XXII issued a papal decree in which he quoted, approvingly, a sixth-century philosopher Boethius as saying, "A person who is intrinsically sensuous will delight in hearing these indecent melodies, and one who listens to them frequently will be weakened thereby and lose his virility of soul."

• With regard to music, the reformer John Calvin endorsed an opinion, which he attributed to Plato, that "there is scarcely anything in the world which is more capable of turning or moving this way and that the morals of men."

• Alan Lomax, quoted earlier in this chapter, wrote of the reinforcing effect of unison singing in a culture that values discipline and conformity:

> Considerable discipline and conformity are enforced by social unison, for all participants must agree that for a considerable length of time, sometimes for hours, everyone follows the same melodic and textual pathway without notable departures from the main rhythmic pattern.

• An excellent illustration of Proposition II in action comes from a 2001 book written by Renée Cox Lorraine, a musician and university faculty member.[1] She explains that while working with the compositions of the late-Romanticist Richard Wagner (1813–1883), she became aware of a particular association involving a melodic pattern consisting of a sequence of *intervals of a third*.

The association that Lorraine sensed in this pattern was, in her words, somewhere between "love, eroticism, and desire," and "spirituality," depending upon other musical factors. Here is her conclusion:

> My affective reaction to these passages [involving a sequence of thirds] is no doubt enhanced by their extrageneric [i.e., extramusical] associations, and it would seem that these associations would have to do with a militaristic patriotism in the first case and a desire for the perfect love of a blissful marriage in the second. Consciously, I have proclivities toward neither militarism nor marriage. But because I tend to associate third relations [see "intervals of a third" in the Glossary] with a delightful mixture of eroticism and spirituality, the third relations in "National Emblem March" and "O Perfect Love," might be conditioning me to have positive feelings about militarism (or patriotism) and marriage as well.

In Chapter 7, I mentioned musicologist Susan McClary and her conviction that chromaticism is sometimes associated with the "irrational or deviant." This conclusion grew out of her research that focused on a feminist critique of music, including art music. She published her conclusions in the 1991 book, *Feminine Endings: Music, Gender, and Sexuality*.[2] In it she expressed an insight that I believe to be of profound importance for our topic of congregational singing. She wrote:

1. Lorraine, Renée Cox. *Music, Tendencies, and Inhibitions: Reflections on a Theory of Leonard Meyer*. Lanham, MD: Scarecrow Press, 2001.
2. McClary, Susan. *Feminine Endings: Music, Gender, and Sexuality*. Minneapolis: University of Minnesota Press, 2002.

> Moreover, music does not just passively reflect society; it also serves as a public forum within which various models of gender organization (along with many other aspects of social life) are asserted, adopted, contested, and negotiated.

A clearer statement of the persuasive power of music would be difficult to find. Professor McClary is not alone in her view of music as a public forum in which ideas regarding a host of social, political, and—we would add—theological, issues are "asserted, adopted, contested and negotiated." This perspective on music will be central to our conclusions in Chapter 10.

Chapter 9

Implications for the music of worship

The book opened with a discussion of the topic of the music wars that have plagued the evangelical church over the past half-century. Subsequent chapters have explored both the benefits and requirements of congregational singing. In an effort to put this study on firm ground I set forth a definition of *worship* and of *corporate worship*, as well as four principles, primarily rooted in Jesus's admonition that worship must be in spirit and truth.

Our attention then turned to two technical aspects of music, namely, the ways in which music can arouse emotions in the listener, and methods by which music conveys meaning through external references. In Chapter 8, the discussion was narrowed to the case which focused on the external references that are attitudes, or values, especially those that are of defining importance to adherents of a group that is a subgroup of a larger culture.

After exploring the relationship between group values and the musical style espoused by the group, I stated two propositions based on the view of many musicologists and ethnomusicologists that a group's music reflects, reinforces, and promotes the core values of that group:

Proposition I: *The core values of a group are supported by the music it espouses.*

Proposition II: *The values supported by a musical style tend to be adopted by, or reinforced in, those who are avid listeners of it.*

It is time now to take all that has gone before and draw out implications for the music used in congregational singing.

Two basic requirements

While there is much more that can be said about the music of congregational singing, there are two requirements that provide clear guidance for the resolution of the music wars. Each is firmly rooted in the work of previous chapters.

Note that these are only "requirements," conditions that discussions in previous chapters show to be *necessary* for the musical style to be acceptable for worship. These two requirements, however, are not *sufficient* criteria for a style to be acceptable for worship. In other words, even if the musical style satisfies the two requirements—as it must—there may be other conditions that need to be met as well. For example, the music of a song might meet the requirements, and even have an excellent text, but the melody or rhythm might be too difficult for a congregation to sing, or, the music might be insufferably dull (there are many examples of this in every style).

After a brief statement and discussion of these two requirements, I will evaluate the degree to which each is satisfied by three common styles of music used in evangelical worship today: contemporary Christian; gospel song; and, classic hymn. (These terms will be clarified below.)

These categories are not exhaustive—there are many songs that do not fit neatly into any one of them. For example, some people use the label "gospel hymn" for songs that have one or more of the features of a gospel song (such as a lengthy chorus), but are more like a classic hymn in other ways (more stately, often having a more moderate tempo and minimal use of the skipping rhythm). (*Great*

Is Thy Faithfulness is one of numerous examples.) In reality, each song being considered for a service must be evaluated individually, not retained or rejected just because of its alleged membership in one category or another.

The purpose in limiting the discussion to the three styles is not only that these three are well-known, but also that they afford a good opportunity to apply the two basic requirements mentioned in this section without our becoming bogged down in extraneous details of one song or another.

The first requirement is that *the music must not introduce into worship values that distort, or are directly contrary to, the truth of God.* Any such introduction would constitute a direct violation of Principle II—that worship must consist of the truth of God—and, for many in the congregation, a violation of truthfulness (Principle III) as well.

Consider this hypothetical situation. The scene is an evangelical service where, as is commonly done today, messages and song texts are projected onto a large screen. Without the knowledge of anyone else, whether in the leadership or the congregation, the person responsible for preparing and executing the projections decides to include, during the songs, repeated subliminal images that are morally offensive. Since no one in the room, other than this scoundrel, will be consciously aware of what is going on, will the worship of the sincere and innocent churchgoer be adversely affected?

Remember that "*subliminal*" means here that the image is presented for such a brief time (a few milliseconds) that no one consciously sees the picture, and so is unable to tell what it depicts. All that might be noticed is a flicker on the screen. Can this imaging possibly affect one's worship? As countless experiments have shown, the image *is* perceived sub-consciously, and can indeed influence people's judgment, attitude, and goals without their being aware of that influence.

So, Principle I (worship must be in spirit) appears to require the conclusion that as part of worship, that activity has been corrupted because the worshipers' minds have been infiltrated by thoughts offensive to God.

One more note. The projected images need not be morally offensive. If they are alien to the text of the song, some degree of confusion in the mind of the singer is probably unavoidable, again a violation of Principle I.

This hypothetical scenario is actually a parable. In what way? The subliminal images correspond to the values communicated in music that, likewise, are perceived at a sub-conscious level. The music itself is heard consciously, but the values embedded in it are generally not, unless they obviously conflict with our understanding of the text, as in the case of "O Sacred Head" sung to Webb.

But whether consciously or sub-consciously perceived, if the values conveyed by the music are in conflict with the truth of God, then this first requirement of this section for determining if the music of a certain song is acceptable in worship has not been satisfied.

It is not sufficient, however, that the music be free of values alien to the truth of God. Why is this not adequate? We have seen that unless the music accompanying a text *supports* the correct interpretation and appropriate emotional response then the singing is detrimental to worship. Congregational *readings* are, at best, problematic, but if we add the burden of singing music that is incongruent with the text, then the situation is made worse.

This leads to the second requirement: *the music must support the values represented in the text of the song*. When you read the examples to be given below, it is important to bear in mind that, over time, worship—including, of course, congregational singing—should span the revealed truth of God (Principle II). It follows that this second requirement imposes a substantial burden on the style(s) of music used to accompany the singing: taken together, they must support values across the full range of revealed truth, including, of course, those having to do with the person and work of God.

Evaluation of contemporary Christian music

The goal in this section is to see how well contemporary Christian music meets the two requirements just discussed. Of course, it is first necessary to establish what is meant here by "*contemporary Christian music (CCM)*." The problem with using the popular abbreviation "*CCM*" is that it means different things to different people. In this book CCM refers to music intended for congregational singing that very much resembles the music that, in recent memory, has been heavily used in the secular popular culture. The usual accompanying instruments and performance characteristics are considered to be part of the music.

CCM will, therefore, convey the core values of one or more popular secular groups. Efforts have been made to "tone down" certain obviously offensive aspects of the music to make it more acceptable to the older generation of churchgoers, but the values are so deeply embedded in the music that this attempt to purge the secular style is difficult to accomplish without destroying the appeal of the music to its adherents.

And what are some of those values? To answer that question we must consider certain values that are core values of modern popular culture in general, and, therefore, that are supported (perhaps in different ways) by all the secular music styles popular today. We will look at four such values, each of which is offensive to God and His gospel. As we do so, we will attempt to identify some musical characteristics that help communicate that particular value.

First is the value of *egocentrism*: according to popular culture, the individual is supreme. Although a very old value of fallen humanity, recent decades have seen increasingly broad and intense public expression of it in the Western world. At every level of society we see rebellion, as the individual rejects authority in favor of self-expression. Traditional social mores, the lessons of history, the wisdom of the elderly, even faithfulness to one's vows—all are set aside as the individual declares himself/herself autonomous.

Undoubtedly, the culture's most obvious musical expression of egocentrism has been rock, as demonstrated in the rock concerts by the counter-culture in the 1960s, and in numerous variations since then. The performance characteristics (such as loud, aggressive music, accompanied by physical gestures that would, in their day, at least, be considered obscene by many people) and the common behavior of the listening audience (exhibiting unrestrained, often illegal behavior, encouraged by the music, for example) bespeak defiance of social and political norms.

A second core value of popular secular culture is, like egocentrism, very old, but has enjoyed a significant renaissance in recent decades. It is *hedonism*, the thirst for pleasure, the desire to be entertained, and the wish, simply, to have fun. Hedonists find special delight in challenging a rule and appearing to get away with it. The rule might be of human origin (e.g., the speed limits), a law of nature (e.g., gravity, challenged in extreme sports), social convention (e.g., standards of acceptable conversation), or of divine origin (e.g., sexual purity or respect for the property of others).

An interesting observation by the musicologist Theo van Leeuwen, is that when the polyrhythmicality (multiple rhythms sounding simultaneously) of African music is carried over to Western music with its tradition of a regular metronomic beat, a new association results. The presence of more than one rhythm represents a subversion of the traditional beat of Western music, and therefore contributes to a weakening of the discipline of the clock (the "law" represented by the regular beat of traditional Western music) and of the work ethic. This change, perhaps sub-consciously, encourages a greater interest in the pleasure that fills one's leisure time.

The easiest example of this phenomenon is syncopation, which introduces a very limited form of polyrhythmicality. By its very nature it challenges the established beat accent pattern that is tied to the clock, and, in van Leeuwen's view, leads to an increase of interest in pleasure rather than work.

Changing the perspective slightly, we can view syncopation as a defiance of the established accent pattern, the "law" of the music, so to speak. As such it amounts to (i.e., is associated with) a "petty transgression" without any penalty, but it is a transgression nevertheless. In other words, syncopation—in cooperation with other musical dimensions—can be associated with hedonism.

I find it interesting to note the rapid and parallel growth of hedonism and loud, heavily syncopated music in the popular culture for more than a century. It is not difficult to believe that the emphatic syncopation common in CCM is supporting the alarming shift of attitude toward worship, suggesting that worship is a time for entertainment of the congregation.

A third core value of today's secular culture is *superficiality*, a preference for that which is intellectually shallow, lacking the substance appropriate to the topic. Implicitly, superficiality denigrates the subject by suggesting that it is not worth deeper consideration. An emotional arousal deserves the designation "superficial" if it is not in agreement with the thinking of the individual at the moment. It might be very intense but merely be the result of overdone expressive effects in the music (as discussed in Chapter 5), or by gestures that suggest a deep moving of one's spirit—a well-timed tear in the eye, rapid and/or loud speech, emphatic movements of the arms, the closing of one's eyes as if in deep contemplation, etc.

Superficiality in worship is utterly offensive to the person of God and the unfathomable depths and surpassing importance of His truth. If superficiality is so foreign to the truth of God, we should be especially concerned to recognize it in the songs that we sing in worship.

It is quite easy to detect superficiality in the text of a song, but how is it communicated in the music? I have already mentioned that loud, heavily-syncopated music is associated with playfulness, hence suggesting that the text ought not to be taken too seriously. The same conclusion can be drawn when an excellent text is accompanied by music that does not fit it well. Excessively simple or repetitive melody, harmony, or rhythm contributes a sense of superficiality as well.

A final example of a core value in today's culture is *sentimentality*, meaning the inclination to deny or ignore aspects of truth, or reality, that are inconvenient, harsh, or unpleasant. In his book,

Faking it: The sentimentalisation of modern society, editor Peter Mullen has gathered scholarly articles that show sentimentality in a variety of human activities: the arts; literature; politics; political science; theology; educational philosophy; and even medicine.

From the pulpit as well as in texts of congregational songs, sentimentalism has led to the "massaging" of the gospel to make it more acceptable to modern tastes. Topics such as sin, judgment, and eternal punishment, are deemed offensive and counter-productive to the evangelistic mission of the church and are therefore slighted.

How is sentimentality supported in the music of a song? When a stimulus is perceived (even sub-consciously), we determine within a half-second whether the stimulus is positive or negative, "friend or foe," so to speak. This is called the "valence" of the stimulus. Research has shown countless times that when a person is "primed" by a stimulus whose valence is unambiguous (e.g., a smiling face is often used for a positive stimulus or a frowning face for a negative), and then the person is immediately presented with another stimulus whose valence may be ambiguous, the person tends to give it the same valence as that of the preceding priming stimulus.

Suppose, for example, one is primed with a distinctly positive feeling, and then is presented with the word "*father*." Many people have mixed feelings about their father, but having been positively primed, they will tend to overlook the negative memories and reflect on the happier times. In effect, the positive feeling that arises sub-consciously from the priming, is misattributed to the memory of father.

We have already seen an example of this in Lafferty's, *Seek Ye First*. The lullaby-like music primes the singer positively, thus encouraging a view of the kingdom of God that obscures the hardship and pain that believers will inevitably encounter.

In my judgment, these examples suffice to show that CCM introduces alien values into worship, and, therefore, fails to meet the first requirement for the music of a congregational song.

It is interesting that among those who are opposed to CCM, its shortcomings on this first requirement seem to garner the most attention. Briefly put, many critics feel that CCM is just too much like secular popular music (its loudness, the choice of instruments, and the behavior of the worship team, etc.). From my perspective, though, the second requirement presents to CCM an even greater challenge.

Recall that the second requirement insists that the music must support the values represented in the text. Given our definition of worship, the values should regard primarily the person and work of God. Among these values are majesty, gravity, awe and respect, divine sovereign authority, omnipotence, divine love, holiness, genuine sorrow, eternality, sin, heartfelt repentance, wrath, judgment and salvation, as well as genuine joy and certain hope. *Since these are not core values of secular popular culture, the culture's music will not support them.* If the culture's music did support these values, then—according to Proposition II—the culture would, at least sub-consciously, adopt them. In short, CCM fails miserably on the second requirement.

Since CCM scores so poorly on both requirements, we conclude that contemporary Christian music—as we have defined it: music, instrumentation, and performance that very much resemble the music, instrumentation, and performance that have been heavily used in the secular popular culture within recent memory—is not suited to worship in spirit and truth.

Evaluation of the gospel song genre

Defining "*gospel song*" is not easy. Many American evangelicals regard it as just another name for the traditional hymn. This view is not surprising since gospel songs and classic hymns are found side-by-side in most song books. A casual glance suggests that there are no differences in the music except that one might have a lengthy chorus. But significant differences do exist.

The songs we call "gospel songs" date mostly from the nineteenth century. The music is usually in a major key, with an "upbeat" tempo. They have attractive melodies that are easy to sing and remember, and simple, repetitive harmonies. They usually have an extended chorus, and often involve the "skipping rhythm" (Chapter 7). An American genre, the gospel song has roots in the classic hymn genre commonly used in the seventeenth and eighteenth centuries in psalters and for the texts of Isaac Watts, Charles Wesley, and others. The gospel song has also been influenced by the campmeeting songs that flourished on the American frontier in the early nineteenth century.

How does the gospel song genre fare when looked at through the lens of the first requirement, namely, that the music (including performance) not introduce alien values into the worship service? The early campmeeting songs were often taken from a growing collection of Christian folk music that borrowed rather indiscriminately from the popular secular culture of the day. But the sieve of time and additional refinement by countless composers, yielded a genre that more faithfully supports the core values of that subgroup of the evangelical church that continues to use the gospel song for its worship.

Those core values that endured from the early nineteenth century through the middle of the twentieth, include revivalism, strong emotion, an antipathy toward formal theological systems, an aversion to the ancient creeds of the Church, and a strong millennial interest. *Egalitarianism* and the rejection of an educated clergy—two more core values that permeated evangelicalism in the early nineteenth century—had largely disappeared by the end of the nineteenth century.

What undesirable values does the gospel song support? The strong emotional impulse in the music suggests that the worshiper's enjoyment is a key element in congregational singing. Indeed, in churches that rely heavily on gospel songs in worship, a song that lacks that emotional force is viewed as dreary. To make the enjoyment of the worshiper paramount, however, is to grossly distort the purpose of worship and to introduce elements of egocentrism and hedonism.

Since the gospel song was developed largely within the church and parachurch organizations like the YMCA and Sunday School movement (rather than the popular secular culture), and since the egalitarianism of the early nineteenth century had passed, one would not expect to find support in the music for any form of rebellion, defiance, or anti-authoritarianism. And I know of no examples of such.

More subtly, however, the earlier rejection of an educated clergy and the strong disinterest in theological systems, including historic creeds, have given some legitimacy to the charge that anti-intellectualism is a group value among that segment of the evangelical church that is satisfied with the gospel song. It would be anticipated, then, that the music of the gospel song supports superficiality, and such is the case. Superficiality is clearly evident in the simplicity of the music (not to mention that of the texts), and in the use of a lengthy chorus that necessarily interrupts any serious development of thought from verse to verse in the text. An excellent example of this can be experienced by singing all five verses of Watts's "Alas! and Did My Savior Bleed," to the tune Martyrdom, and then singing the gospel song version composed by Ralph E. Hudson (1842–1901), *At the Cross*. (The piano accompaniments are available at www.neusong.com.)

Sentimentalism—either denying unpleasant aspects of reality, or (its other meaning), mushy emotionalism—is another negative value supported by the gospel song through its frequent association with happiness and its high emotional impulse. A careless use of chromaticism and other expressive devices often adds a syrupy sentimental sense. Both forms of sentimentalism compromise the truth of God.

Superficiality and sentimentalism are significant alien values supported by the gospel song genre. But it does not appear to engender ungodly thoughts (conscious or sub-conscious). A low passing grade on the first requirement seems reasonable.

On the second requirement—that the music support the text of the song—the picture for the gospel song is not all negative. For some texts, especially ones having to do with praise of God for what He has done (e.g., Fanny Crosby's (1820–1915) "To God Be the Glory"), or, the certainty of heaven (e.g., another Fanny Crosby text, "Blessed Assurance") or a call to zealous Christian service (e.g., Sabine Baring-Gould's (1834–1924) "Onward, Christian Soldiers"), a gospel song can be supportive.

But there are many subjects of worship for which the gospel song genre is woefully inadequate. An easy example is the core Christian value of genuine sorrow for sin. The gospel song's skipping rhythm, its almost exclusive use of major key tonality, and the up-beat tempo bespeak happiness rather than sorrow. The result is that lines such as, "Years I spent in vanity and pride, caring not my Lord was crucified," and "I was sinking deep in sin, far from the peaceful shore," are rendered in a most inappropriate, gleeful setting.

Equally difficult to support in the gospel song genre are texts dealing with the nature of God, His majesty and power, as well as the gravity, awe, and reverence that should characterize congregational response.

We would expect that of all the core values of evangelical Christianity, the one that should be supported by their chosen musical style is the bodily resurrection of Christ. Yet, very few gospel songs are devoted to the topic. Why? As shown in Robert Lowry's (1826–1899) *Christ Arose*, a favorite of many, the gospel song style will support the imagery of a physical resurrection (especially seen in the first phrases of the chorus), but this falls short of the substance that a mature Christian congregation should express regarding the resurrection. The superficiality of the style will not support a robust declaration thereof. (For contrast, study "Christ the Lord is Risen Today," and see how well the traditional hymn tune, Easter Hymn, supports this grand text by Charles Wesley.)

More evidence exists, but clearly the gospel song is severely limited in its ability to support texts having to do with the nature of

God. The gospel song is somewhat better with texts that speak of the elements of redemption or the general Christian experience, for example. Given the origin and development of the gospel song—campmeetings, churches, Sunday school, the YMCA—none of this is surprising. A weak passing grade on the second requirement is probably appropriate.

Evaluation of the classic hymn tune

The hymn tune for congregational singing can be traced back to the Bohemian Brethren, followers of John Hus (1369–1415), in the opening years of the sixteenth century. In 1505, they published a hymn book that is said to have contained about four hundred hymns, with melodies. The hymn tune as we know it gradually evolved over several centuries, as did the congregation's participation in singing, the use of instrumental accompaniment, and the tempo at which the songs were sung. At first the songs (even Luther's majestic "A Mighty Fortress Is Our God") were sung in a sprightly "rhythmic" style, with liberal use of what sounds to us like syncopation. For a variety of reasons the rhythmic style yielded, over time, to the "*isometric*" form that we have come to associate with typical eighteenth and nineteenth century congregational singing. The four-part harmonies with which we are familiar were known in the sixteenth century; but unison singing prevailed until at least the eighteenth century.

What exactly are the characteristics of the "classic" hymn tune that is the focus of this section? The classic hymn tune is usually written with multiple "voices" or parts, only one of which—the "melody"—is primary, with the others playing supporting roles. This genre is meant to be sung by a group of untrained singers, often in unison. This expected lack of training implies that the melody should not be difficult to sing; the rhythm relatively simple; and the tempo, steady and moderate, being neither too slow nor too fast. When appropriate to the text, as in the expression of sorrow, music in a minor key is not unusual. The composer is free to make limited use of dissonance; in that case, simplicity in singing usually requires the congregation to sing in unison.

A hymn tune is intended to accompany a text of substance, so the music should not convey any hint of superficiality and should be free of tawdry devices that inevitably draw attention to themselves and away from the text. A classic hymn tune is generally expected to use chromaticism with great discretion and to avoid any suggestion of mushy sentimentalism. The rhythm should not encourage inappropriate movement of the body.

Finally—and very importantly—the hymn tune is meant to be sung in the worship of God, and so should be seen by the outside-the-church culture as dignified and having appropriate gravitas, but not necessarily somber.

This is a somewhat imprecise description of what I understand to be required of a "classic" hymn tune. It is left to the reader to see how CCM and the gospel song genre fail to meet this description. The classic hymn tune for congregational singing was honed over a period of almost five hundred years. Its development has been influenced by folk and art music, as well as by the growing availability of instruments for accompaniment, notably, the organ. Composers representing a variety of protestant theological persuasions have not only contributed their own original works but have also modified existing tunes to accommodate patterns of congregational singing and changing associations (as in Luther's Ein Feste Burg (*A Mighty Fortress*)). The result is that the classic hymn tune—unlike its offshoot, the gospel song—cannot be considered the group music of a narrow segment of Protestantism. In fact, the values communicated by the music tend to be those of the historic church of the Reformation.

So, how well does the classic hymn tune meet the criteria of the first requirement for a congregational song? The foregoing discussion provides a partial answer. First, the style appears to be free of values that would be out of place in worship that is in spirit and truth, but that does not imply that the style is forever fixed. In recent decades new tunes have been composed that give greater emphasis to dissonance and rhythm, but do so in a way that seems to be appropriate to worship and support of the text, not merely as entertainment.

It is possible for a tune to seem like other hymn tunes but to support unsuitable values. One example is the Maori tune, mentioned in Chapter 5. It looks like a hymn tune, but it is heavily larded with chromaticisms, making it highly sentimental, as befits a farewell song. Not surprisingly, in mid-twentieth century the tune was used for the secular text, "Now Is the Hour When We Must Say, 'Good-bye.'" The music is most unsuited to the Orr text, "Cleanse Me, O God," and to Christian worship in general.

But there is another important observation that supports a high grade on this first requirement: *It is clear that the popular secular culture has largely avoided the classic hymn style.* This fact suggests that the style does not communicate the values of that culture.

What about the second requirement? Is the classic hymn tune genre able to support the full range of revealed truth? The fact that the style is still used for many of the Western world's serious patriotic songs suggests that, even though it has fallen into disuse in much of the evangelical church, this style continues to connote reverence, gravity, honor, and majesty in the larger culture. This is a pretty good start toward a high grade on the second requirement.

Furthermore, for more than three centuries the classic hymn has maintained a fairly constant form. To judge the classic hymn tune on the second requirement, one has only to examine the numerous hymnals used in those evangelical churches that did not follow the populist movement in its adoption of the gospel song. The topical indices will reveal a wide range of subject matter, and for most of the songs listed, the music will be of the hymn genre and will be supportive of the texts. It is interesting to note that the translations of the early texts on the resurrection are invariably set to classic hymn tunes. The other styles we've looked at will not bear the weight of such substantive texts.

Of course, just because the music of a given song is of the classic hymn style, doesn't mean that it is suitable to that text. In many cases, the tune used was not written for that particular text, and so the support might not be as strong as it could, and should, be. A case in point is How's stirring text, "For All the Saints." The hymn tune, Sarum, by Joseph Barnby has been used but it is only weakly supportive of the text. The tune Sine Nomine composed by Ralph Vaughan Williams specifically for this text is vastly superior and far more supportive. Sine Nomine matches the boldness, confidence, and triumphant sense of the text, whereas Sarum conveys a more tentative, subdued joy.

Clearly the hymn tune form can adequately support texts across the full spectrum of God's truth. So, the evidence considered from the perspective of these two requirements points to the conclusion that the classic hymn tune genre is far superior to both CCM and the gospel song genre for use in congregational singing.

Chapter 10

A different perspective on the music wars

It is probably safe to say that the music wars that have plagued and perplexed the evangelical church for the past half-century are commonly seen as an inter-generational conflict over musical taste and preference. Having spent many hours listening to secular popular music, young people find the traditional music of congregational singing lacking in excitement, while the older generation tends to see contemporary music as unsuited to worship. We have all heard the arguments on both sides so many times that this description of the conflict seems indisputable.

Or is it? Certainly this assessment of the problem is not wrong, but I believe it to be dangerously superficial. The purpose of this final chapter is to suggest a different perspective, one that should give pause to all who love Christ and His Church.

A (hopefully) deeper analysis

It is interesting to think about how completely the evangelical church has capitulated to the young people's musical preferences Why has this happened? The first response one is likely to hear is probably along the lines of "If a church doesn't appeal to the younger generation, then they will go elsewhere and that local church will ultimately cease to exist."

As though to bolster this initial response that seems weak, one usually hears a follow-up argument like this, "The important thing is that by using their style of music we get the young people into the church to hear the preaching of God's Word. Besides, if the words are ok, what difference does the music make? Granted, the older folk won't be happy with it, but they will probably conclude that this is the way life goes and that they'll have to get used to it."

Notice the crucial assumption in that response: if the words are ok, then the music makes no difference. This is the reason this widely-held view has been mentioned numerous times in this book. If the assumption is correct then the several compromises that the church has chosen as solutions are understandable, although it is lamentable that such a significant part of the congregation is left dissatisfied.

But—as I have sought to show in these pages—the assumption that the music makes no difference, is *not* correct. The growing conviction among ethnomusicologists and musicologists is that music—the music itself, not merely the words—can convey values. In the forefront of this movement have been musicologists who personally prefer, and who are currently studying, popular music.

One of the leaders in the "new" musicology is Prof. Susan McClary. In her 1991 book, *Feminine Endings: Music, Gender, and Sexuality*, she undertook to show how music—even famous (read "serious") music of the nineteenth century communicated negative messages about women, homosexuals, and others. In Chapter 8, the following passage from McClary's book was quoted:

> Moreover, music does not just passively reflect society; it also serves as a public forum within which various models of gender organization (along

with many other aspects of social life) are asserted, adopted, contested, and negotiated.

I firmly believe that this view—that in society, music functions as a public forum—is true for models of theological perspective in the "public forum" of congregational singing. By this is meant that congregational singing, for good or ill, offers a forum in which different views of the nature and work of God, the Church, and worship itself, are "asserted, adopted, contested, and negotiated."

What follows are insights arising from two authors who—in different parts of the twentieth century—made astute observations about the American evangelical church. Neither author made any explicit connection with the music that the church had adopted, but it seems clear that their assessments fit very well with my conclusions that arise out of musical considerations.

A. W. Tozer: The Knowledge of the Holy

The first author, A. W. Tozer (1897–1963), was a pastor in the Christian and Missionary Alliance Church for forty-four years. Through his preaching and writing he gained considerable stature in the evangelical church in the first half of the twentieth century. In 1961, shortly before his death, he published *The Knowledge of the Holy: The Attributes of God; Their Meaning in the Christian Life.* You may remember that I began this book with a quotation from Tozer's Preface, and I repeat it here. He wrote:

> The message of this book does not grow out of these times but it is appropriate to them. It is called forth by a condition which has existed in the Church for some years and is steadily growing worse. I refer to the loss of the concept of majesty from the popular religious mind. The Church has surrendered her once lofty concept of God and has substituted for it one so low, so ignoble, as to be utterly unworthy of thinking, worshipping men. This she has done not deliberately, but little by little and without her knowledge; and her very

unawareness only makes her situation all the more tragic.

Later in the same Preface, Tozer expressed his concern about the loss of "religious awe and consciousness of the divine Presence." The last line of the above quotation offers an arresting commentary: "This she [the church] has done not deliberately, but little by little and without her knowledge; and her very unawareness only makes her situation all the more tragic."

At the time Tozer penned these words, I was a recent college graduate, and I had grown up in one of the finest of evangelical churches of the time. This church, large by the standards of the day, was blessed with strong leadership, a healthy emphasis on basic teaching and evangelism, and unsurpassed zeal for supporting foreign missions. The people of that church were among the finest Christians I have ever known.

But, in retrospect, I see that the church was strong in exactly those values supported by the gospel song genre; but not as strong in their concept of God. In particular, absent was that sense of the *majesty* of God that Tozer saw in the broader evangelical church as well. Respect and godly obedience were hallmarks of the people, but not a strong appreciation of God's great majesty and the awe that we should feel in His presence.

How could this be? It was not until my college years that I realized that I was almost totally ignorant of the life-enriching treasure of Christian hymnody. We sang gospel songs almost exclusively, as did much of the fundamentalist wing of the evangelical church in the first half of the twentieth century. The texts, though true (if not pressed too hard), were actually quite weak, but the music was stirring, and that seemed to make the songs good enough for worship.

Now, in the light of the more recent recognition, by musicologists, of music's persuasive power (which we discussed in Chapter 8) and in light of the awareness that the gospel song genre lacks the capacity to convey majesty (as well as many other aspects of the person and work of God) we have a very plausible explanation for the decline Tozer witnessed. I suggest that it is to be found in the consistent and almost exclusive use of gospel songs.

It might be oversimplifying to claim that the decline in the awareness of the majesty of God—a decline in proper awe before Him, or in a sense of the divine Presence—should be attributed to the preference for the gospel song. But it is possible, even likely, that this claim is, in fact, true. Because of the attractiveness of the gospel song style, especially in its strong emotional appeal, the people virtually required its near-exclusive use in many evangelical churches in the first half of the twentieth century. Over time, the absence of support for such aspects of God as His majesty, etc., led almost imperceptibly ("little by little and without her knowledge") to a decline in the church's awareness thereof. Those who sang a steady diet of gospel songs were denied the necessary refreshment in the majesty of God that well-chosen classic hymns would have made available.

It is interesting to note that the half-century over which Tozer observed the loss of awe for God corresponds roughly to the period between the Moody/Sankey meetings—that had made the gospel song immensely popular—and the time of Tozer's writing.

David Wells: *God in the Wasteland*

Evangelical theologian, seminary professor, and author David F. Wells (b. 1939), offers a second example of a serious decline in the church's conception of God. In his book, *God in the Wasteland: the Reality of Truth in a World of Fading Dreams*, Wells evaluates the state of the church at the end of the twentieth century.[1] His perspective is broader than Tozer's, but the conclusions are remarkably similar. He writes regarding the evangelical church:

> The traditional doctrine of God remains entirely intact while its saliency vanishes. The doctrine is believed, defended, affirmed liturgically, and in

1. Wells, David F. *God in the Wasteland: The Reality of Truth in a World of Fading Dreams*. Grand Rapids: Wm. B. Eerdmans Publishing Co., 1995.

every other way held to be inviolable—but it no longer has the power to shape and to summon that it has had in previous ages.

Now, two decades after the publication of *God in the Wasteland*, one might reasonably consider it much too generous to say that "the traditional doctrine of God remains entirely intact." In the judgment of many, the church's defense of "the traditional doctrine of God" has deteriorated substantially. But even if we accept his more positive statement, the conclusion is devastating. In his description of the evangelical church, Wells declares that "God has become weightless," by which he means "inconsequential."

But how can it be that "the traditional doctrine of God remains entirely intact," when God has become "inconsequential"? If the doctrine is unchanged, then its loss of "the power to shape and to summon" can only mean that those who profess to own that doctrine no longer take it seriously. Does this begin to sound familiar?

In our judgment the weightlessness that Wells ascribes to the present-day evangelical conception of God, is closely tied to the absence of the core values of the Christian faith in the music of congregational singing, chiefly, now, CCM and minor modifications thereof. With music in our church imitating music of the secular world we can't help but be powerfully influenced by the core values of the secular world, values that are quietly screaming at us not to take seriously what remains of "the traditional doctrine of God." For example, music that communicates playfulness— e.g., the loud, heavily-syncopated, music which we mentioned earlier—encourages, even demands, that we treat the text as inconsequential. As we have stated again and again, *the music acts as a commentary on the text*.

Even Wells's characterization of the conception of God as "weightless," brings to mind the sub-conscious work of the music of congregational singing. He wrote:

> Weightlessness is a *condition*, a cognitive and psychological disposition. It can sweep through all

doctrinal defenses because it is not itself perceived to be a doctrine. It can evade the best ecclesiastical defenses, sidestep the best intentions, and survive the most efficacious spiritual techniques because it is not recognized as a kind of belief. Although this weightlessness is not itself a doctrine, it has the power to hobble all doctrines; although it is not an ecclesiology, it can render all ecclesiologies impotent; although it is not itself a spirituality, all spiritualities are withered by its presence.

And, in all likelihood, this unrecognized weightlessness impacts not only the songs that we sing but also all other aspects of our worship. If this is true, then even in churches in which the truth of God is faithfully proclaimed from the pulpit, that truth can be unwittingly, but very effectively, undermined by the music that is such a prominent part of congregational participation. Again, the words of A. W. Tozer seem most apropos:

This she [the church] has done not deliberately, but little by little and without her knowledge; and her very unawareness only makes her situation all the more tragic.

My perspective on the music wars

At the beginning of this chapter I acknowledged that the long-standing musical controversy in the evangelical church can be seen as an inter-generational conflict over musical taste or preference. But I claimed that this is a superficial view.

My perspective is that Satan, the arch-deceiver, has cleverly used the church's true disagreement over musical preferences to obscure the real war that is being fought in the public forum of congregational singing. I believe that although neither side is aware of it, the true war is not over musical style but over the church's view of God. That is to say, the real question that is being—as McClary put it—"contested and negotiated" is not "Whose music will prevail?" but rather, "What conception of God will prevail in His church?"

Using the insights of A. W. Tozer, who did not argue from a musical perspective, I have sought to demonstrate that the exclusive use of the gospel song genre in the early half of the twentieth century weakened the church's conception of God by a loss of the awareness of His majesty, of awe, and of the concept of His divine Presence. Now, a half-century later, David Wells has argued—again, like Tozer, apart from any musical concerns—that in the evangelical church God has become inconsequential. It seems not to matter any more that our holy God abhors sin, that His judgment is certain and eternal, that He demands our obedience, and so much more. I have endeavored to show that, to a significant degree, the church's staggering loss of the conviction that Jesus is Lord, and therefore of utmost consequence, is due in large part to the music of congregational singing.

Yes, the twentieth century witnessed an explosion in Christian songs, yielding volumes of supposed praise of God. But I fear that the church's conception of the one, true, eternal and unchangeable God is, in reality, vanishing.

Glossary

Art music   Art music is a term used to distinguish one of three large categories of music, the other two being folk music and popular, or what some would call "light entertainment" music. By contrast, art music is thought of as "serious" or "advanced," the music of high culture. Many people in Western culture use the term "classical music" when they really mean "art music."

Cadence   "Cadence" is used in this book in two distinctly different ways. The first deals with the rhythmic flow of spoken text, as in congregational readings—the tempo and phrasing of the reading. The second is used in music to speak of any of several patterns of chords that are commonly used to indicate that the music is coming to the end of a phrase or to the end of the composition. In the classic hymn tune and in gospel songs this often corresponds to the end of a musical line.

Cognitive processing   A general phrase referring to the workings of the human mind. Of particular interest in this book is the ability of the mind to improve its processing efficiency by anticipating, from the information available to it, what might be about to happen and to gather its resources in preparation.

Egalitarianism   A belief in equality of all people, usually with regard to certain rights. Its use here is the denial of the existence of an elite clerical class, especially in the late eighteenth and early nineteenth centuries.

Entrainment   The synchronization of self-contained rhythmic processes that are, in some sense, connected. For our purposes, entrainment is the driving of certain muscle groups in the human body into synchrony with the beat of music heard by the individual. A standard example is one's tapping his/her foot to the musical beat.

Evangelistic style accompaniment   A style of piano accompaniment especially suited to the gospel song because of the relatively simple melodic and harmonic structure of that genre. Many different strains have developed, some much more elaborate than others. The basic idea is to fill-in intervals in the melody, or pauses in the music, with "runs" up and/or down the keyboard. It is another expressive effect, demanding considerable technical skill on the part of the pianist. With the virtual demise of the gospel song, "evangelistic playing" is now rarely heard.

The style was perfected by Rudy Atwood (1912–1992), the much-loved pianist of evangelist Charles E. Fuller's (1887–1968) weekly radio broadcast "The Old-Fashioned Revival Hour," heard by millions of faithful listeners in the second quarter of the twentieth century.

Exclusive psalmody   The church policy that allows only inspired texts to be sung in worship. In practice the approved list often consists of the biblical Psalms, the Ten Commandments, and several of the New Testament canticles.

Gospel song   The typical gospel song is similar in appearance to a multi-verse folk song or hymn. It is almost always in a major key and has an "up-beat" tempo. Its most distinctive marks are the frequent presence of an extended chorus, or refrain, that is sung between successive verses, and the use of the so-called "skipping rhythm," which conveys a lightheartedness suggestive of a child's skipping down the sidewalk. The melody is generally attractive, simple and repetitive, easily remembered. The harmony is likewise simple, and repetitive. The texts that are used with gospel songs frequently lack substance. The gospel song genre gained great popularity during the Moody/Sankey revival in the late nineteenth century and was eclipsed by the rise of contemporary Christian music in the 1960s and 1970s.

Hymn tune   The entire musical setting for a congregational song, not just the melody. The phrase is not generally used for contemporary Christian music. Hymn tunes are often given names which can arise from a variety of sources. For example, the hymn tune for the familiar *Doxology* is "Old Hundredth," chosen because the text of the *Doxology* is drawn from Psalm 100. The hymn tune used for *O God Our Help in Ages Past* is known almost everywhere by the name "St. Anne," which is the name of the church in which the composer of the music, thought to be William Croft (1678–1727), was organist.

Interval of a third   A major third consists of four half-steps, while a minor third has three half-steps. John Dykes's (1823–1876) familiar hymn tune Nicaea (*Holy, Holy, Holy*) begins with two consecutive intervals of a third, as does Joseph Barnby's (1838–1896) tune Perfect Love (*O Perfect Love*), which, in days past, was heard regularly at weddings. The *National Emblem March,* mentioned by Lorraine, was composed by Edwin Eugene Bagley (1857–1922). Though not well-known by name, the music is very familiar. It, too, involves intervals of a third prominently in its melody.

Isometric rhythm   A rhythmic form in which there is a well-defined beat, with all time values being fractions or multiples of the beat (e.g., quarter-notes—usually one beat in time—, half-notes—usually two beats long—, eighth-notes—usually half a beat in length. In isometric rhythm the beats are grouped into measures of equal length and the first beat in each measure is accented.

Metricize   To recast a text into the form of a traditional English poem to facilitate its being sung by a congregation. For example, the hymn *All People That on Earth Do Dwell,* is a metricization of Psalm 100.

Misattribution   When the human mind detects, consciously or sub-consciously, a change in the normal state of equilibrium of the body, it immediately attempts to account for it, to attribute it to some source. However, loosely-speaking, the scope of its search is limited to what is within the attention of the individual at that moment. If it appears "reasonable" to the mind that it has found the source, then the attribution is made. Repeated experimentation has shown that the range of "reasonable" and the effects of the attribution are truly astonishing.

It is not unusual, however, for the mind to be fooled, in which case a "misattribution" occurs. This all takes place sub-consciously and very quickly. Our primary interest in this book is the case in which the misattribution is of an emotional nature, the true source being music that is, by one means or another, kept from the attention of the individual (e.g., expressive effects of which the person is unaware).

Musicology   "Musicology" is derived from the Greek words for music and "the study of," hence means the study of music (just as "theology" means the study of God). It does not refer to learning to play an instrument, but rather to "how music works" in the world, both in the individual and in society.

"Ethnomusicology" is that part of musicology that studies music at the cultural level. For example, determining the functions of music within a culture.

Polyphony   A type of musical composition in which there are two or more lines (or "voices," or "melodies") that are more or less independent of one another, but yet together create an harmonious sound. In polyphonic music no one voice dominates above the others, but they are not completely independent, each freely going its own way. Instead, the composer carefully arranges the lines so that they sound well together. For example, the familiar choir descant can be seen as creating a polyphonic setting of one verse of a hymn tune.

Polyphony is different from the usual hymnic form (called "homophony") in which there is one line identified as the melody, with the other lines playing a supporting role. The supporting lines are usually known today as "alto," "tenor," and "bass."

Polyphony appears to have arisen in church music in about the tenth century AD.

Psalter   A collection of metricized Psalms.

Subliminal   A term loosely used to refer to a stimulus that is not consciously perceived but yet is influential in the mental processing of the individual. In our use of the term, the music is clearly heard consciously, but the values conveyed are usually perceived only sub-consciously. We also use it to refer to projected images of such short duration that the viewer is unable to tell that anything has been seen, but yet the image *is* perceived sub-consciously, with possibly powerful impact on the attitude, behavior, etc., of the individual.

Syncopation   A compositional technique that challenges the regular accent pattern by adding emphasis to beats, or fractions thereof, that are not metrically-accented (i.e., not accented by the established metrical pattern), or by removing emphasis from metrically-strong beats. Syncopation is a very powerful emotion-inducing device, one that is used in many contemporary Christian songs. It has been used for centuries in art music, but did not become a fixture in popular music until the piano music of Scott Joplin (c. 1867–1917). In contrast to CCM, very few instances of syncopation are found in gospel songs.

Index